GUITAR TABLATURE EDITION

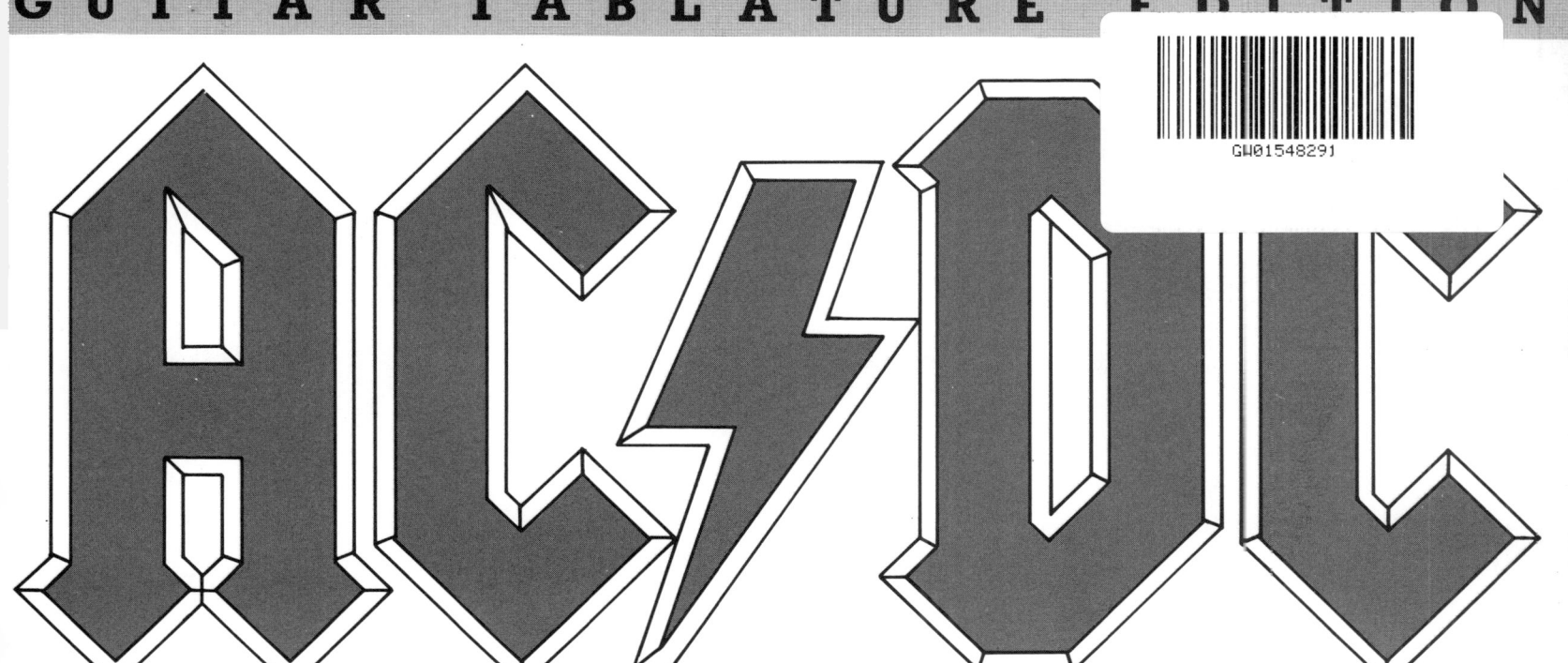

WHO MADE WHO

Amsco Publications
New York/London/Sydney

COVER ARTWORK COURTESY OF ATLANTIC RECORDS
BACK COVER PHOTOS BY GEORGE BODNAR
GUITAR TRANSCRIPTIONS BY RALPH AGRESTA, JEFF CIAMPA, AND JOHN MCCREA
EDITED BY ASKOLD BUK

THIS BOOK COPYRIGHT © 1991 BY AMSCO PUBLICATIONS,
A DIVISION OF MUSIC SALES CORPORATION, NEW YORK

ALL RIGHTS RESERVED. NO PART OF THIS BOOK MAY BE
REPRODUCED IN ANY FORM OR BY ANY ELECTRONIC OR MECHANICAL MEANS,
INCLUDING INFORMATION STORAGE AND RETRIEVAL SYSTEMS,
WITHOUT PERMISSION IN WRITING FROM THE PUBLISHER.

ORDER NO. AM 85556
US INTERNATIONAL STANDARD BOOK NUMBER: 0.8256.1315.9
UK INTERNATIONAL STANDARD BOOK NUMBER: 0.7119.2732.4

EXCLUSIVE DISTRIBUTORS:
MUSIC SALES CORPORATION
225 PARK AVENUE SOUTH, NEW YORK, NEW YORK 10003 USA
MUSIC SALES LIMITED
8/9 FRITH STREET, LONDON W1V 5TZ ENGLAND
MUSIC SALES PTY LIMITED
120 ROTHSCHILD STREET, ROSEBERY, SYDNEY, NSW 2018, AUSTRALIA

PRINTED IN THE UNITED STATES OF AMERICA BY
VICKS LITHOGRAPH AND PRINTING CORPORATION

LEGEND OF MUSICAL SYMBOLS 4
CHASE THE ACE 5
D.T. 26
FOR THOSE ABOUT TO ROCK (WE SALUTE YOU) 66
HELLS BELLS 50
RIDE ON 40
SHAKE YOUR FOUNDATIONS 58
SINK THE PINK 30
WHO MADE WHO 12
YOU SHOOK ME ALL NIGHT LONG 20

LEGEND OF MUSICAL SYMBOLS

CHASE THE ACE
YOUNG/YOUNG

COPYRIGHT © 1986 BY J. ALBERT & SON PTY, LIMITED.
ALL RIGHTS FOR THE U.S. AND CANADA ADMINISTERED BY J. ALBERT & SON (USA) INC., ASCAP.
INTERNATIONAL COPYRIGHT SECURED. ALL RIGHTS RESERVED. USED BY PERMISSION.

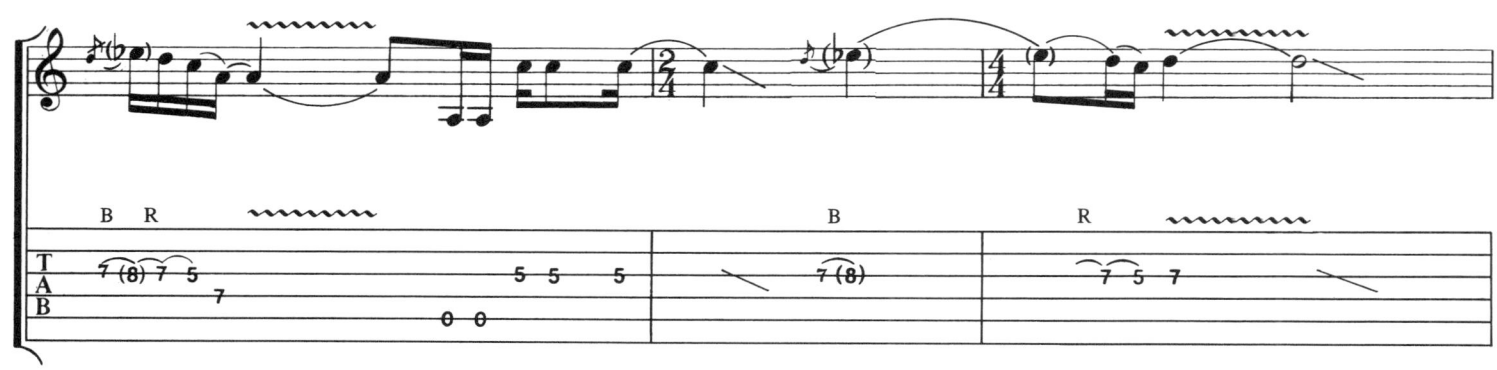

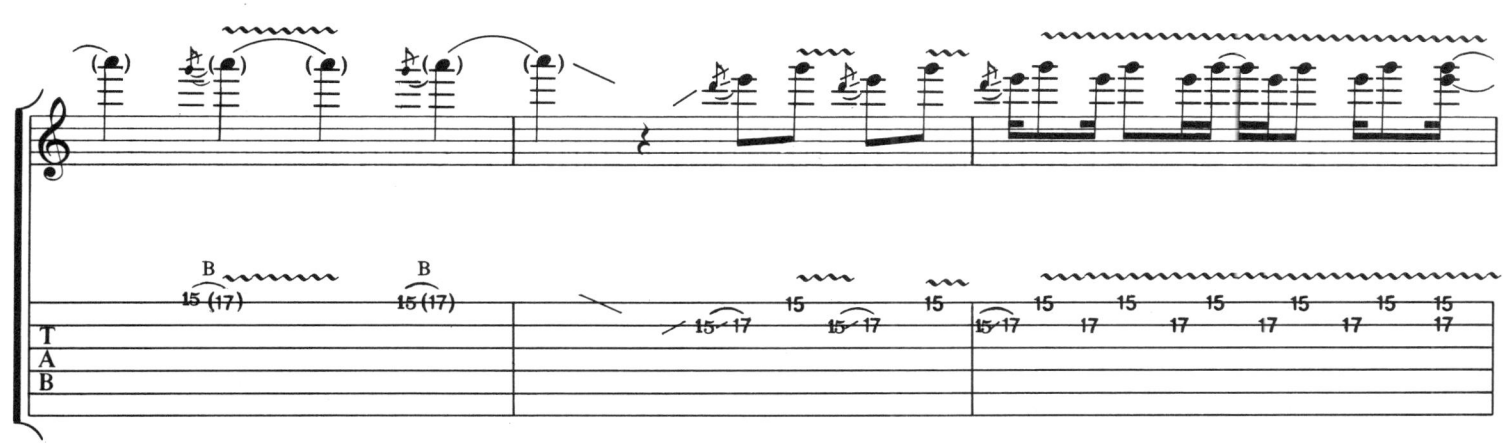

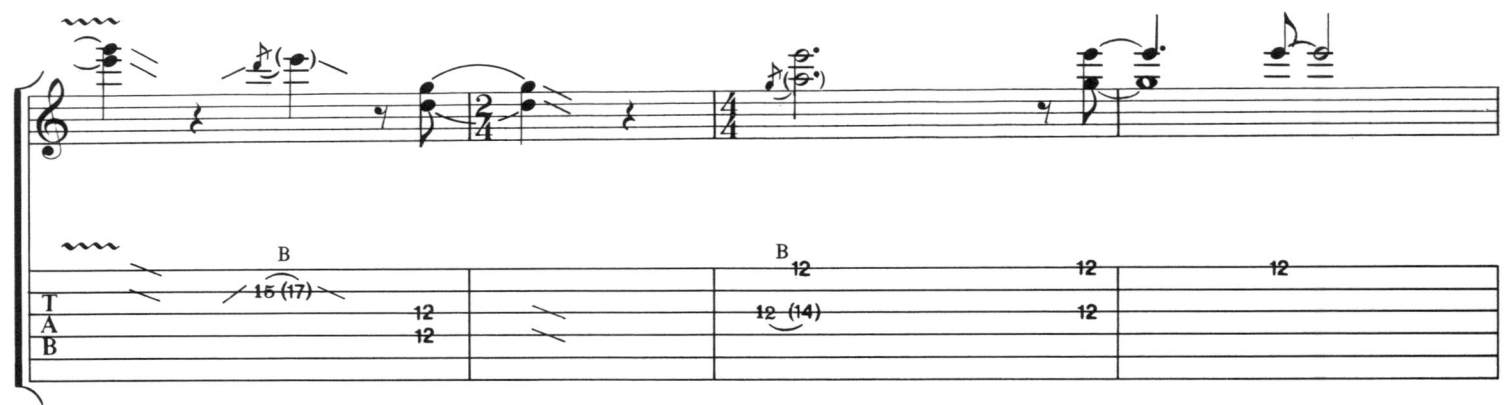

C5 D5 A5
with Rhythm figure 1 and 2 (3 times)
C5 D5 A5
C5 D5 A5
G5 D5
C5
G5

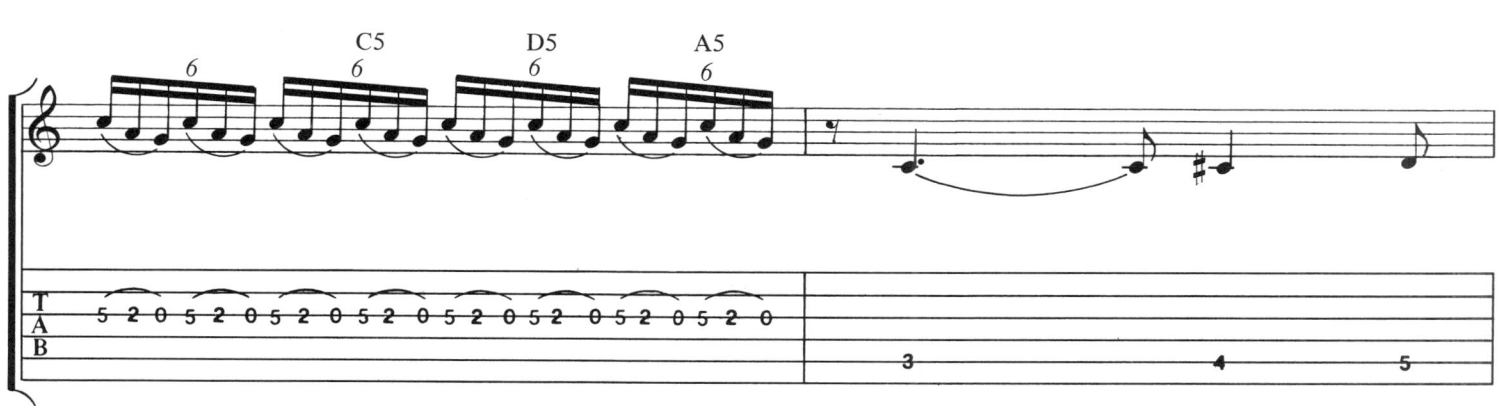

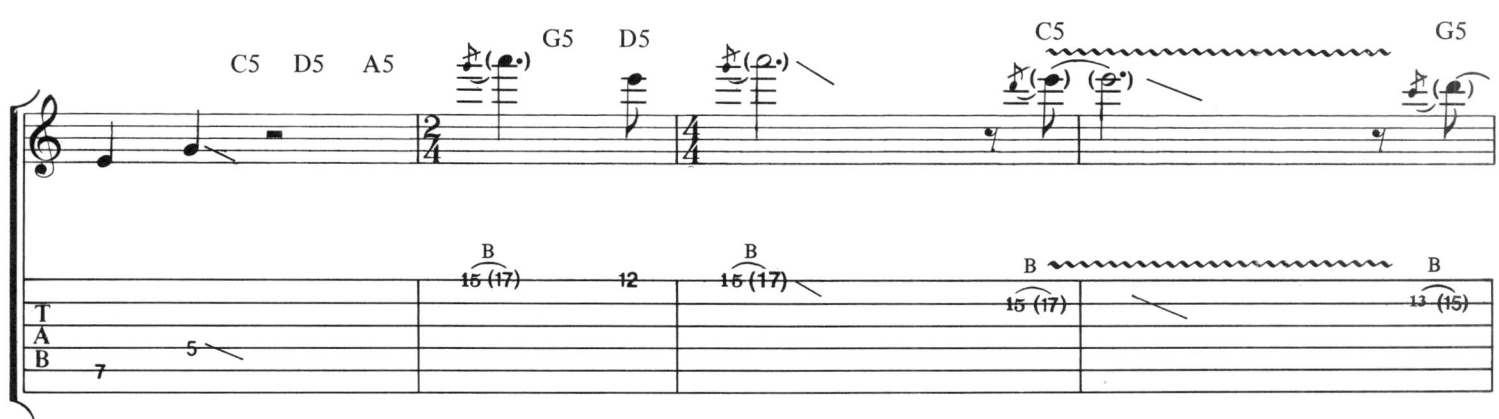

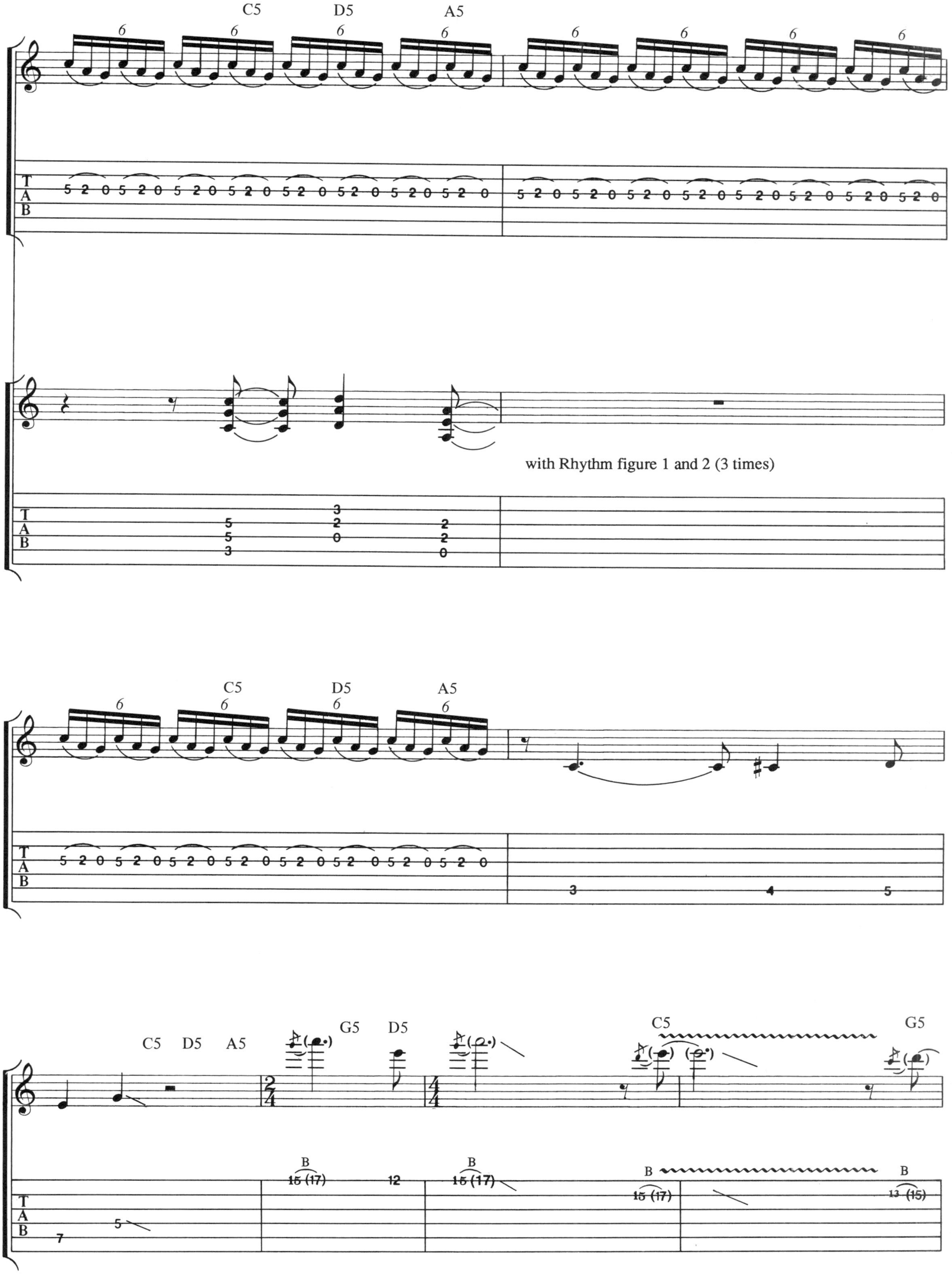

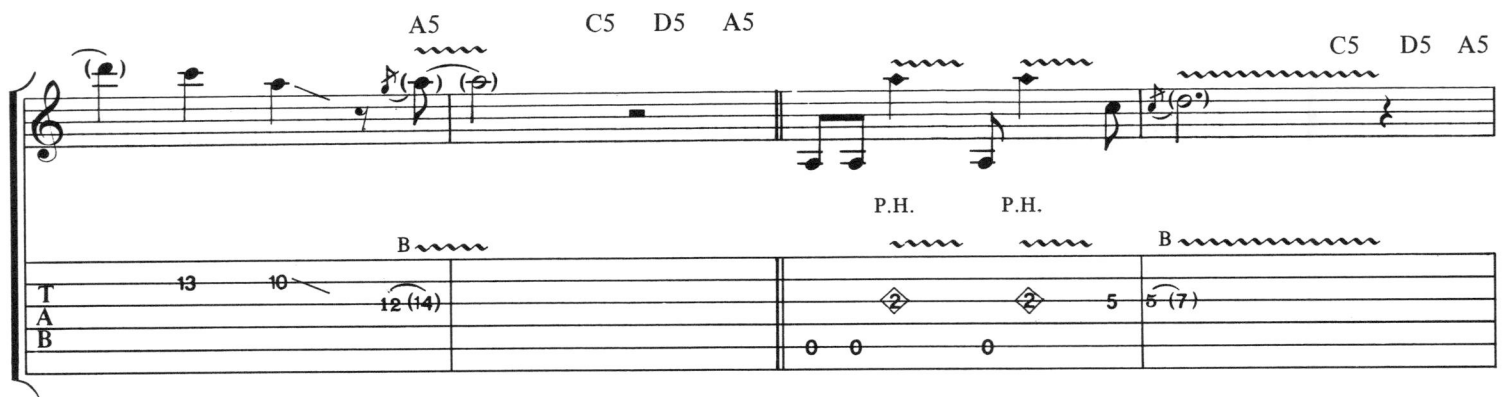

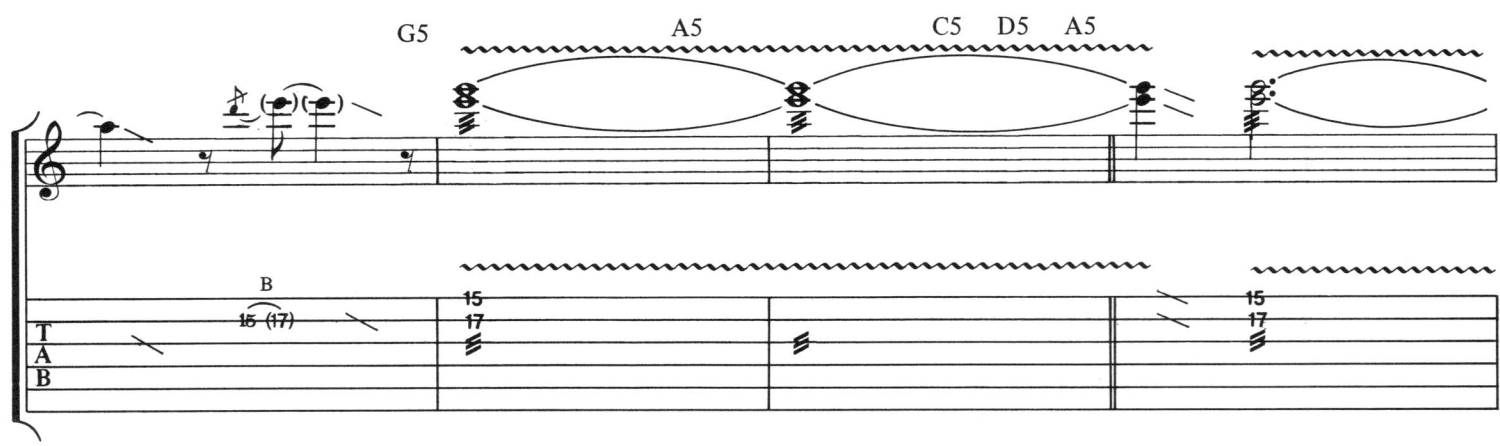
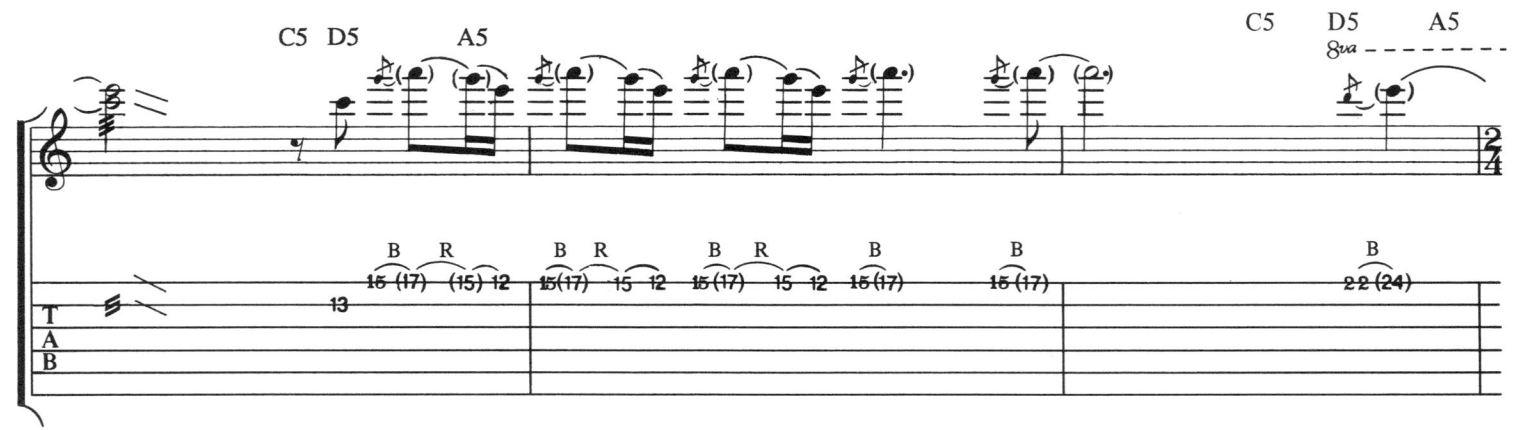

WHO MADE WHO

YOUNG/YOUNG/JOHNSON

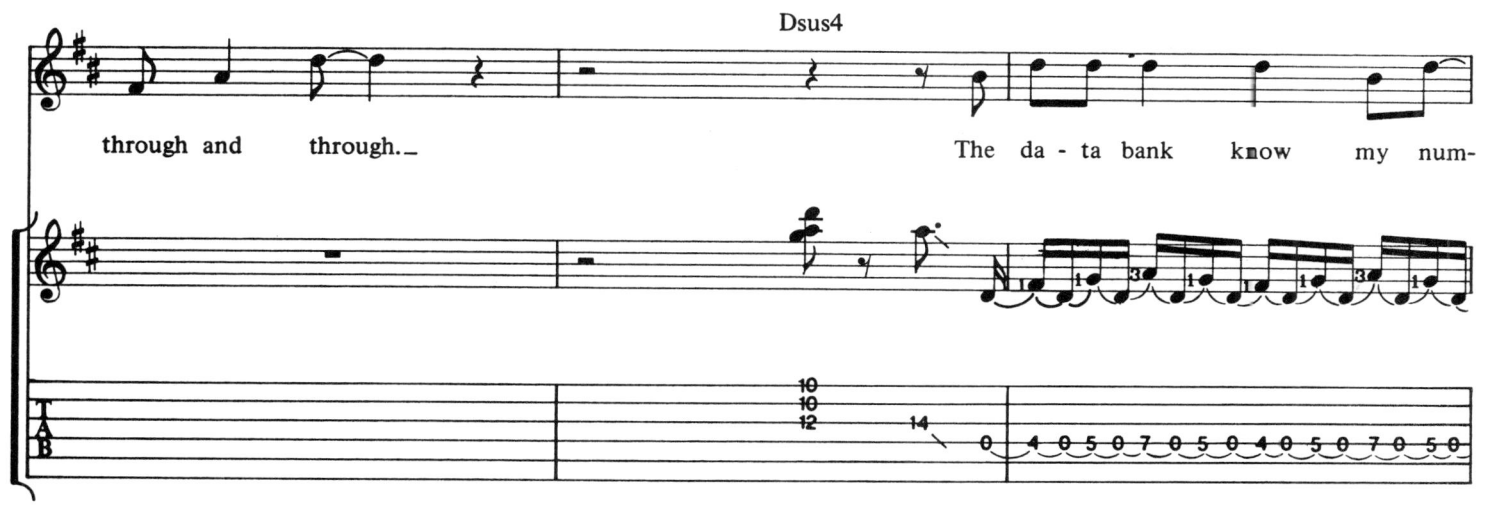

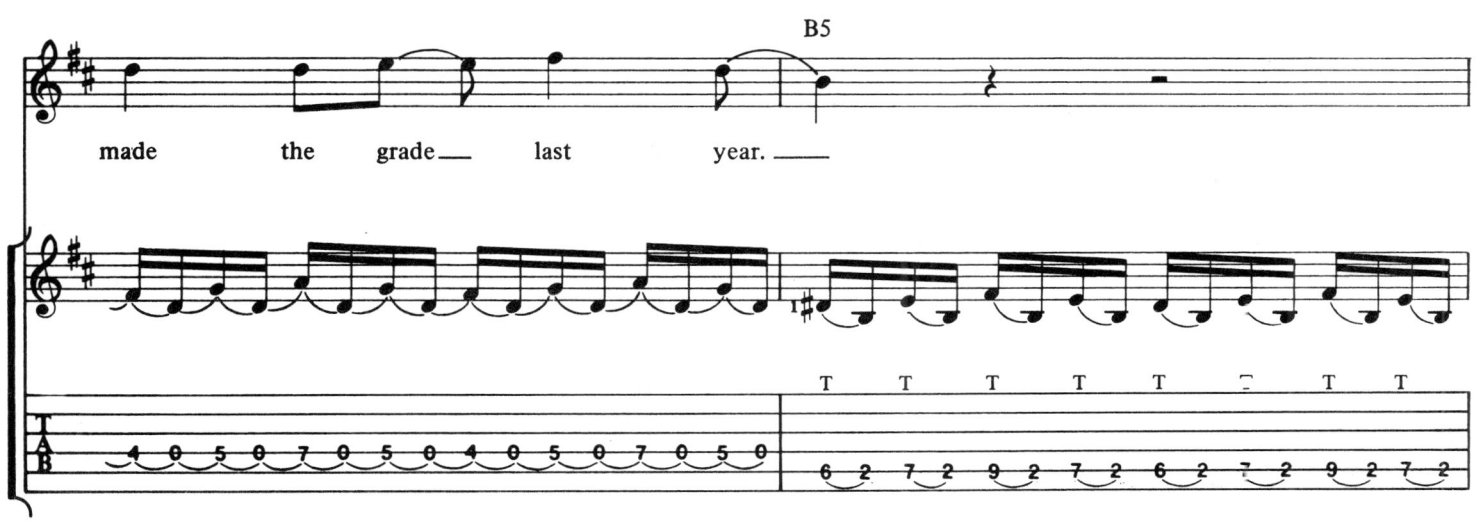

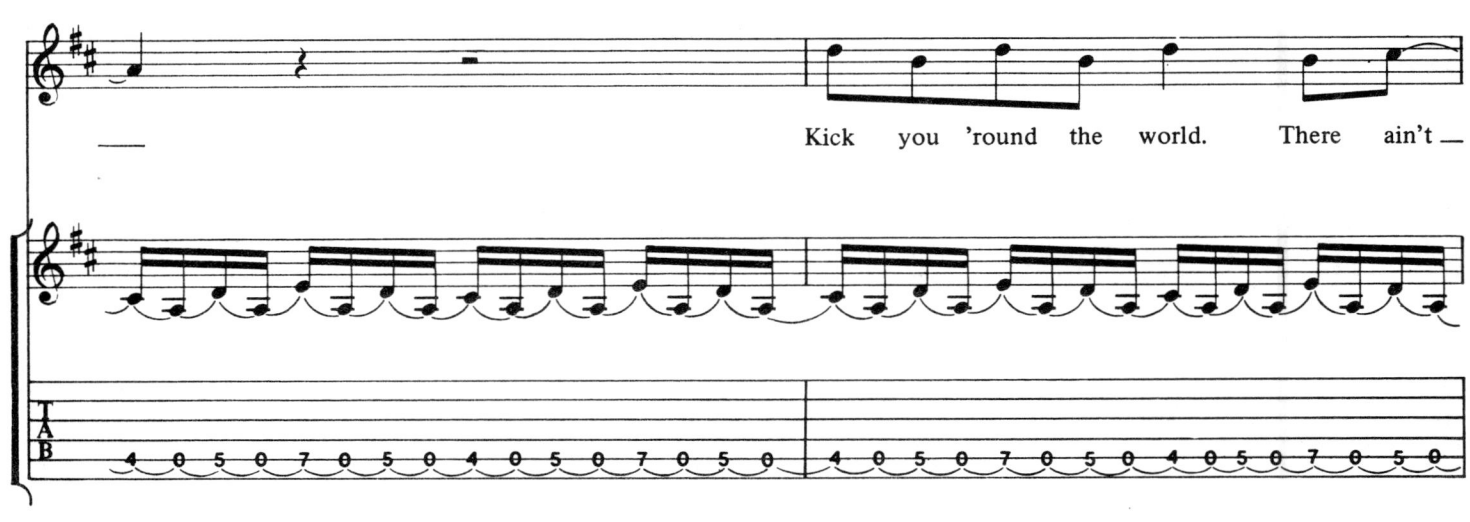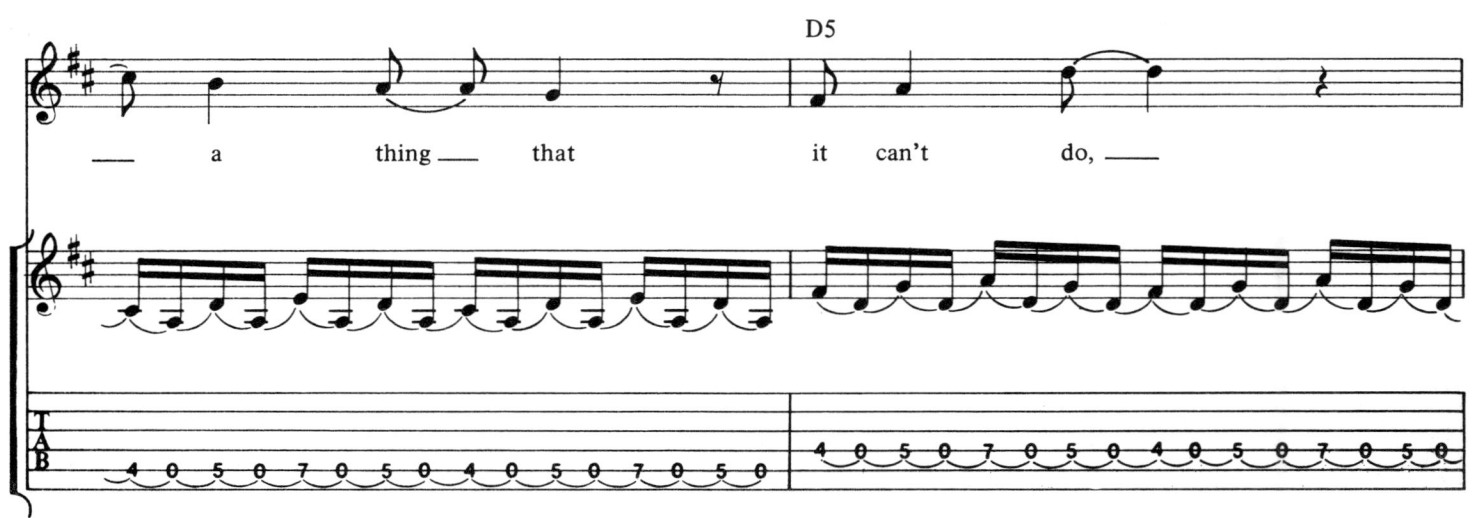

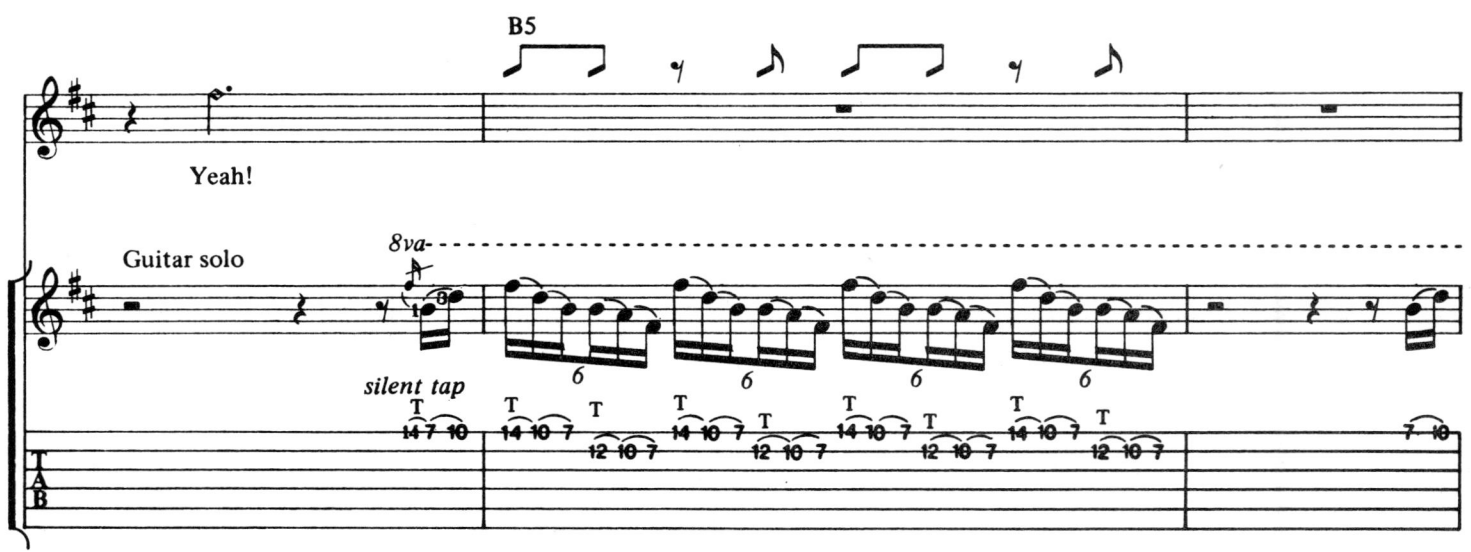

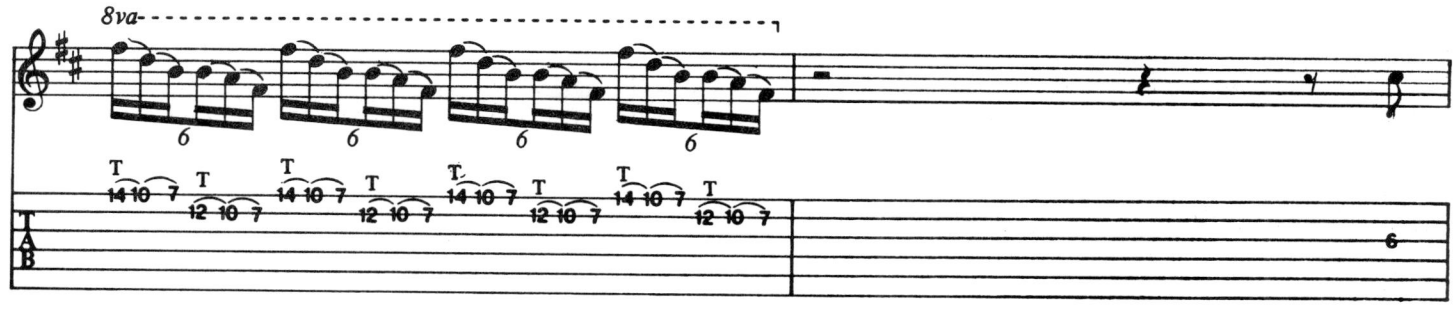
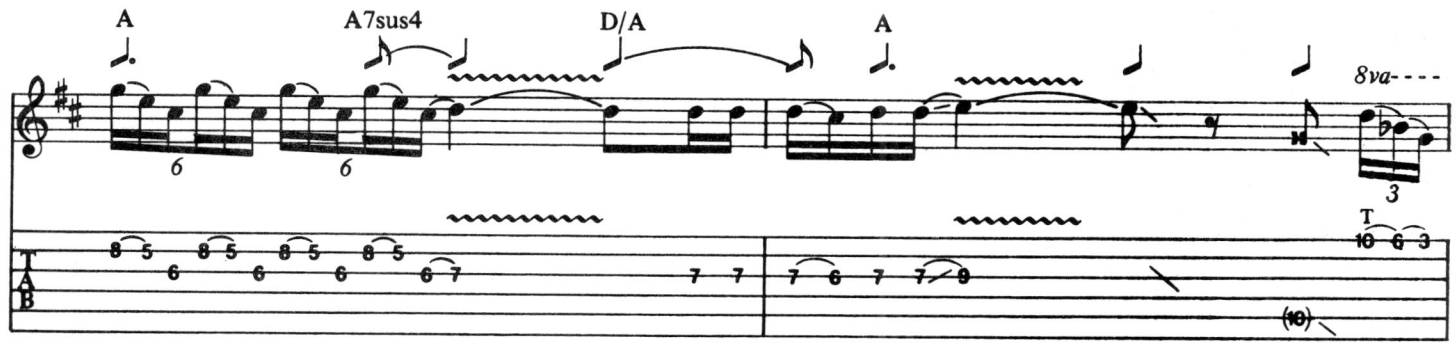

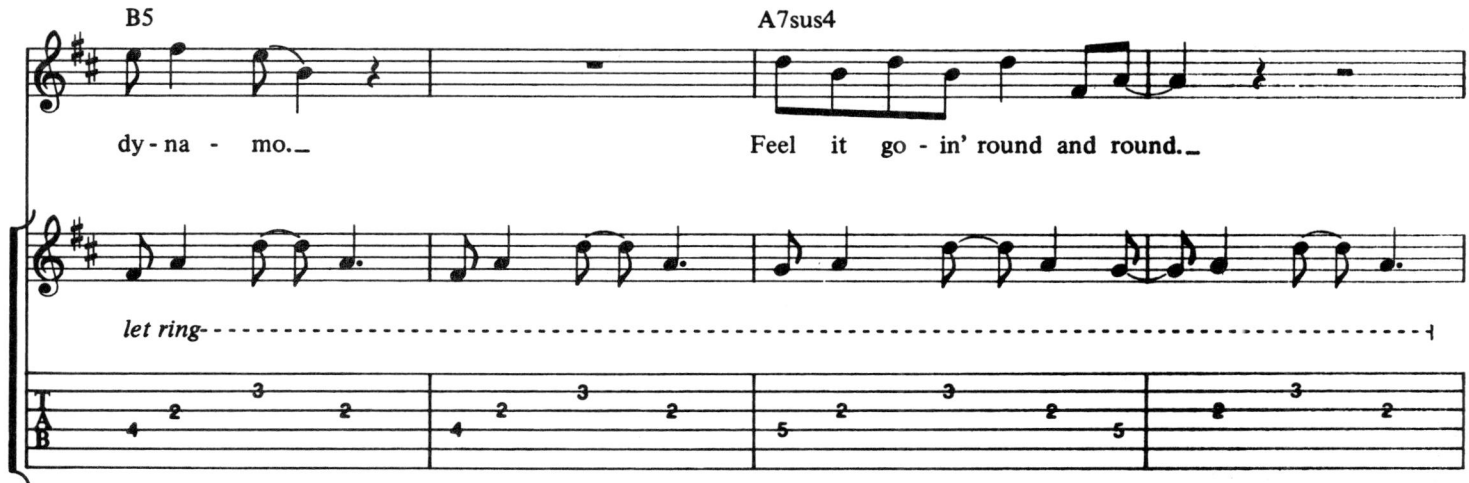

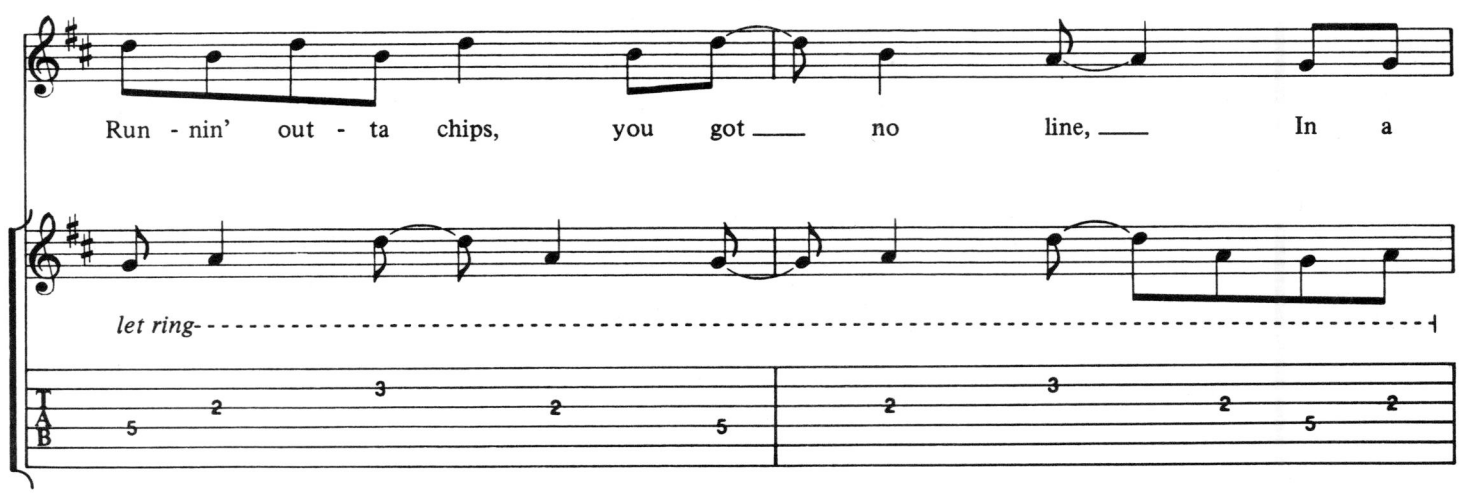
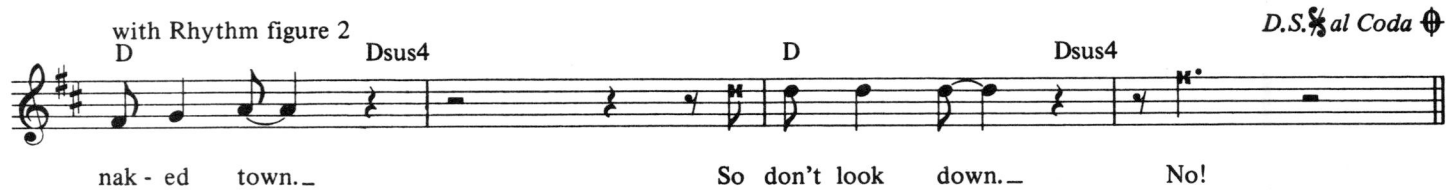

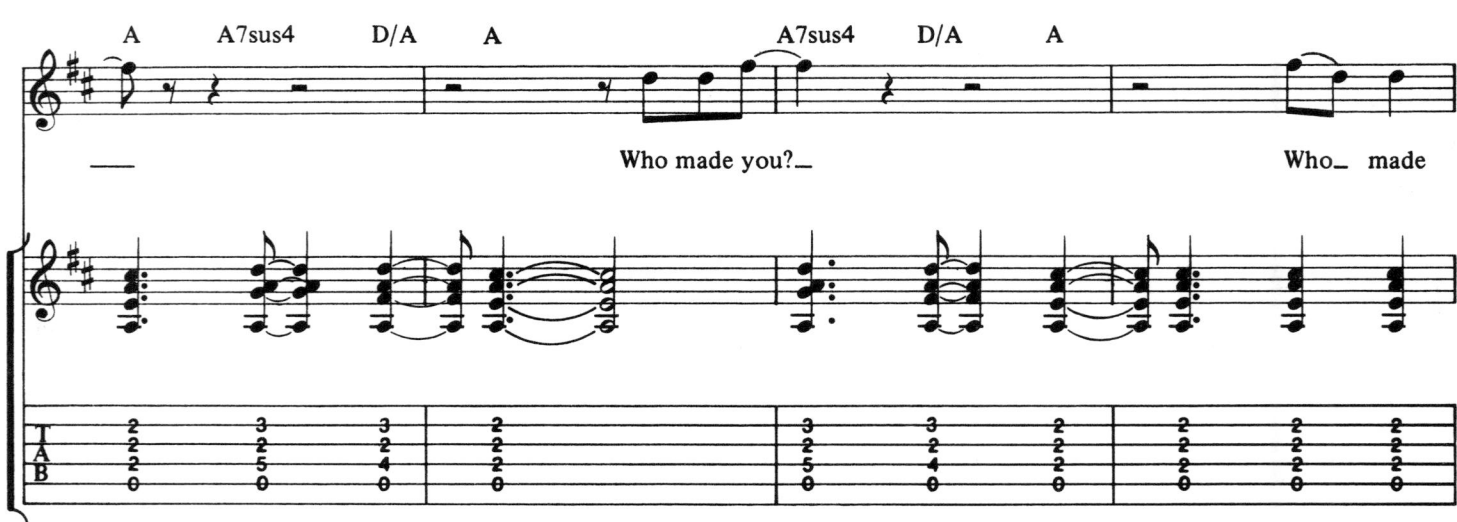

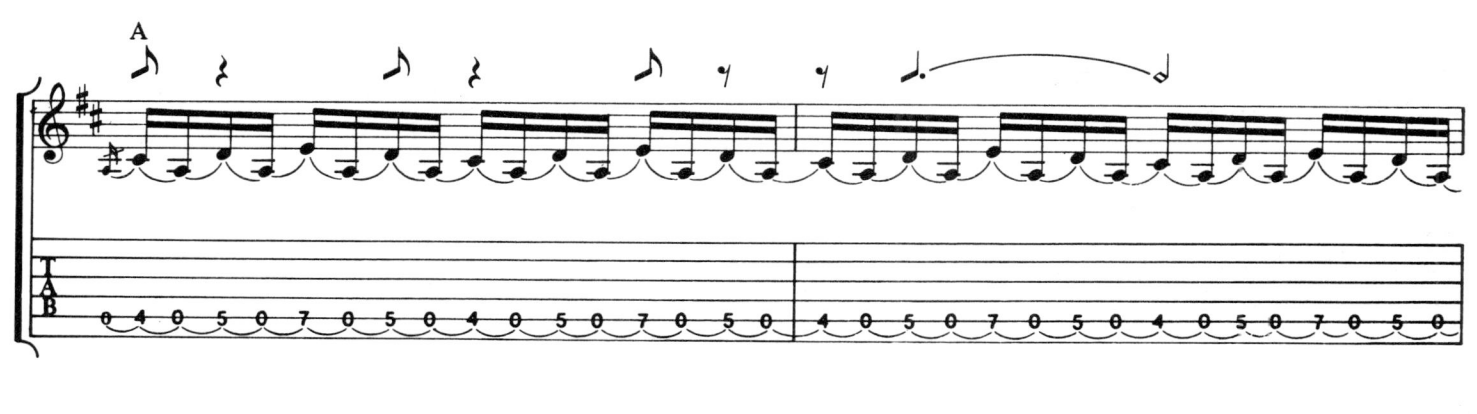
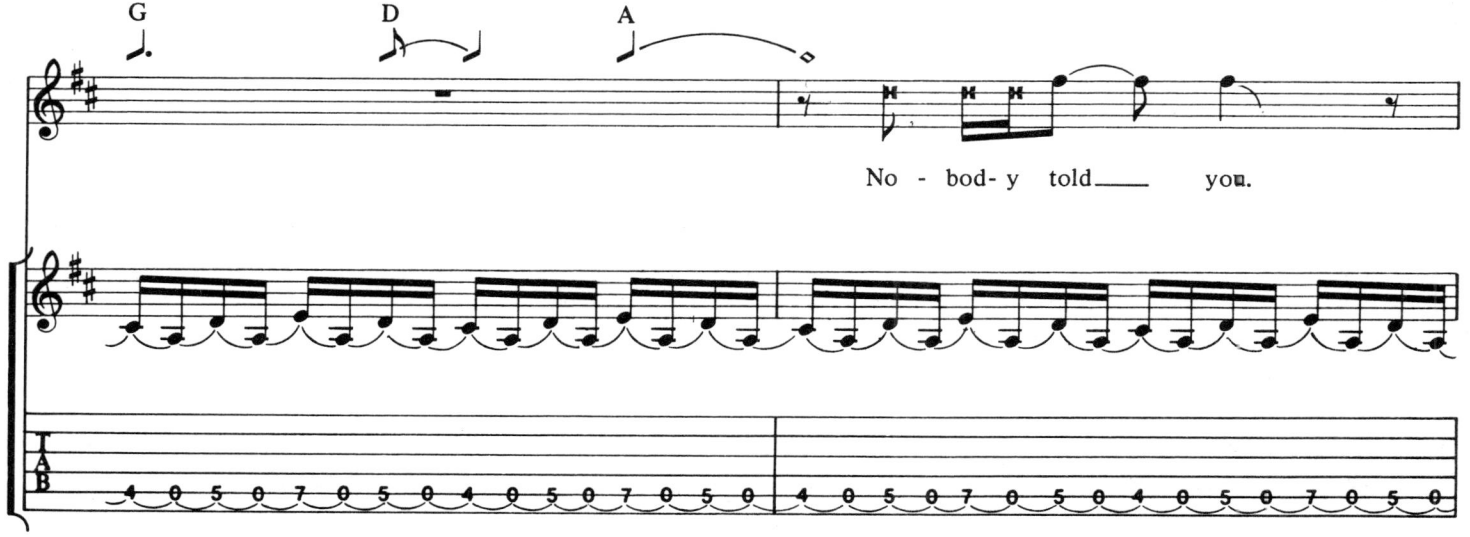
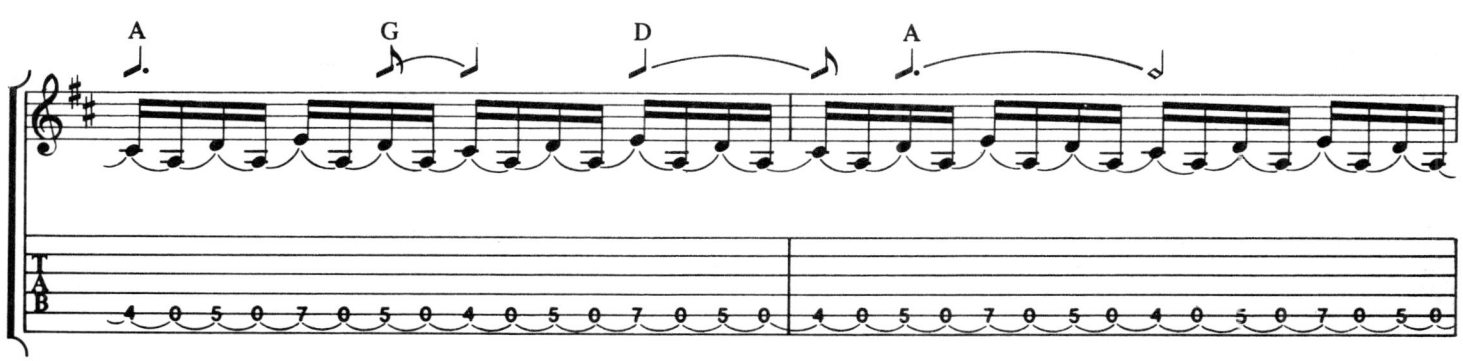
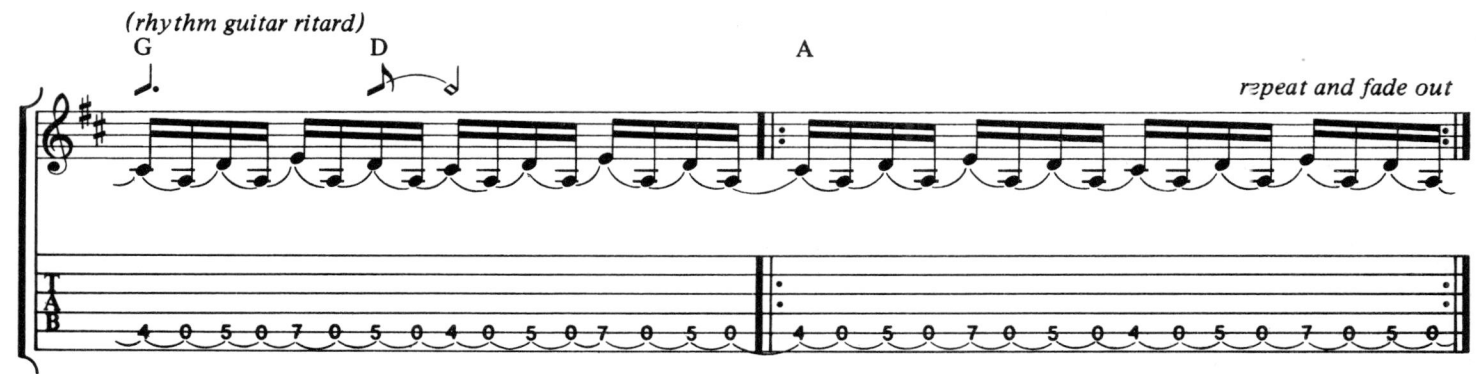

YOU SHOOK ME ALL NIGHT LONG

YOUNG/YOUNG/JOHNSON

COPYRIGHT © 1980 BY J. ALBERT & SON PTY, LIMITED.
ALL RIGHTS FOR THE U.S. AND CANADA ADMINISTERED BY J. ALBERT & SON (USA) INC., ASCAP.
INTERNATIONAL COPYRIGHT SECURED. ALL RIGHTS RESERVED. USED BY PERMISSION.

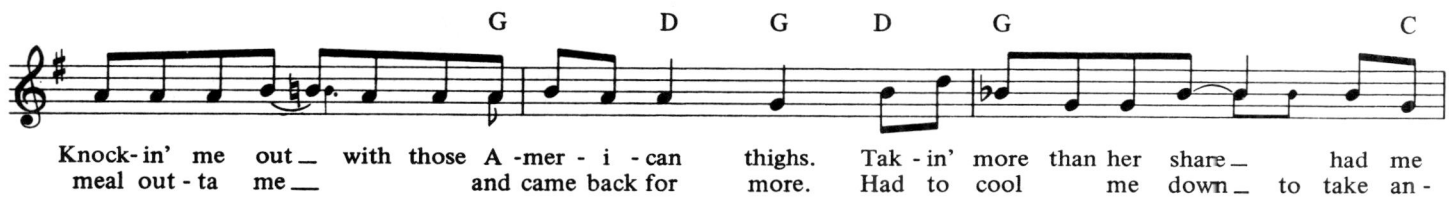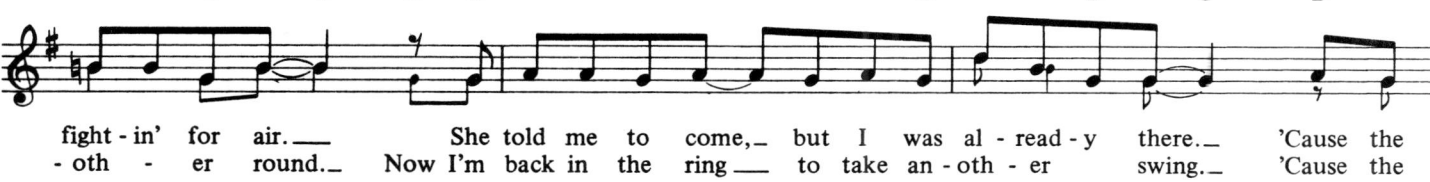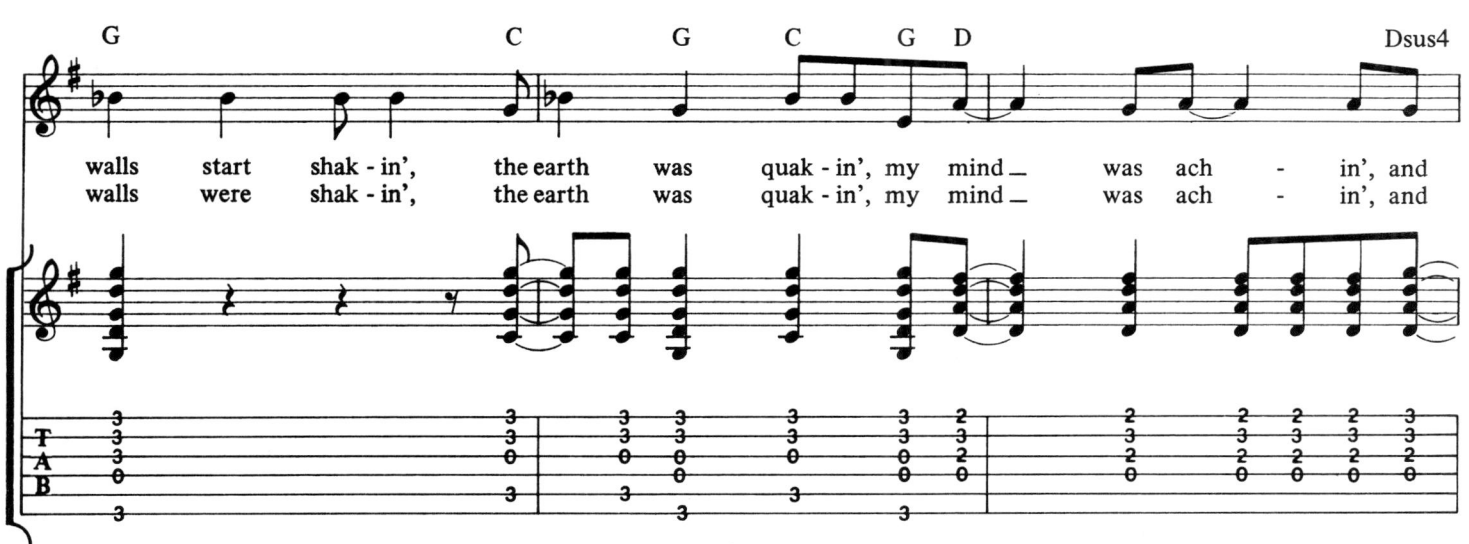

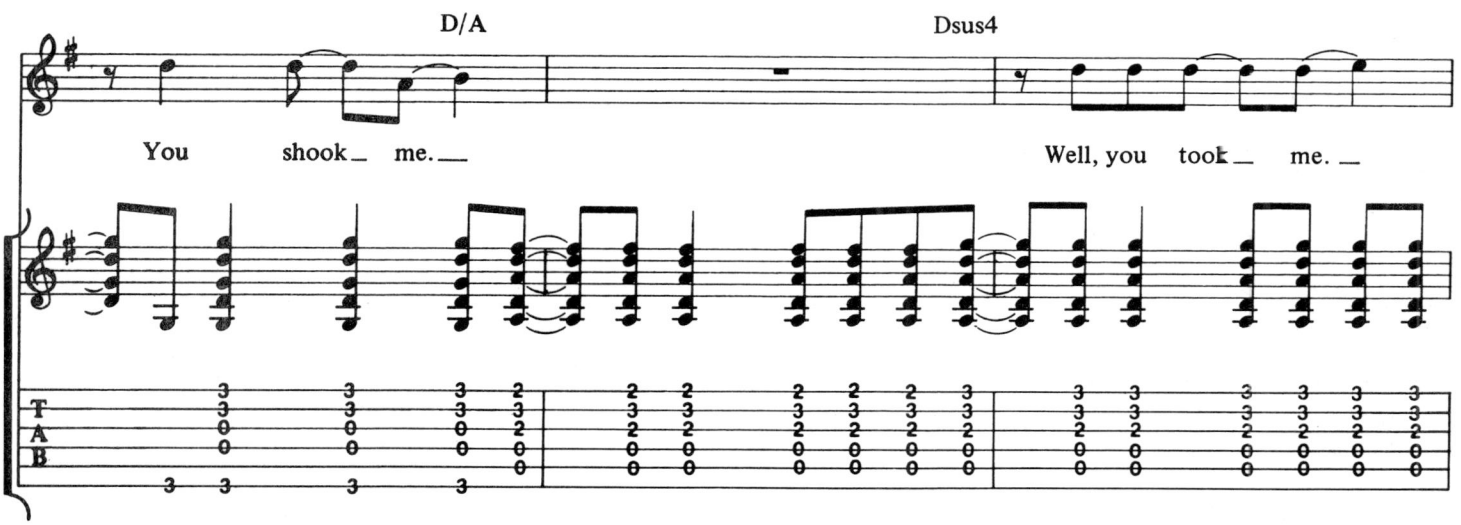
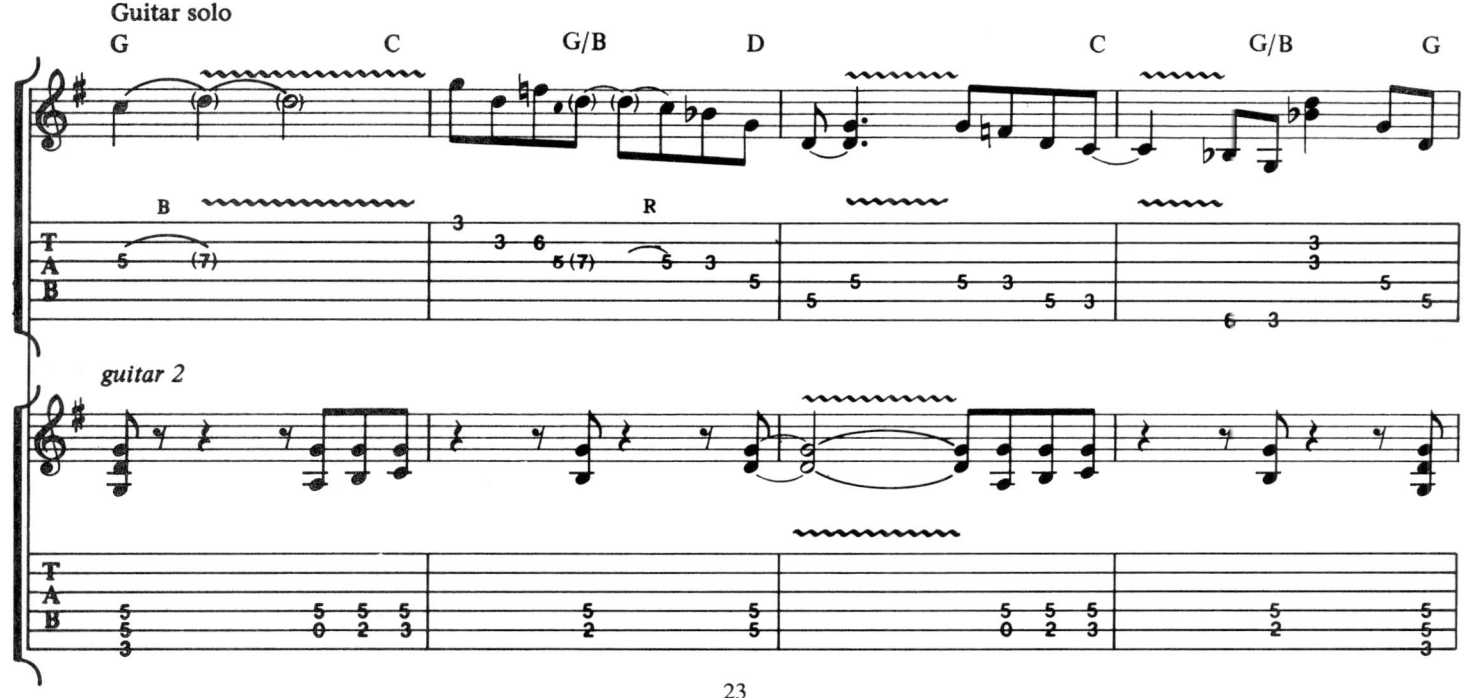

D.T.

YOUNG/YOUNG

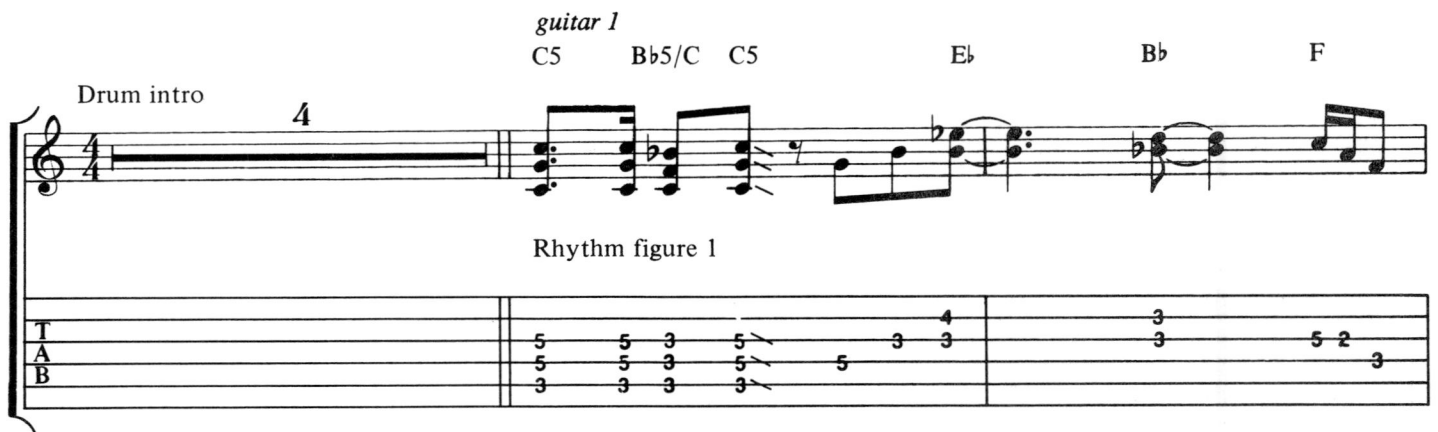

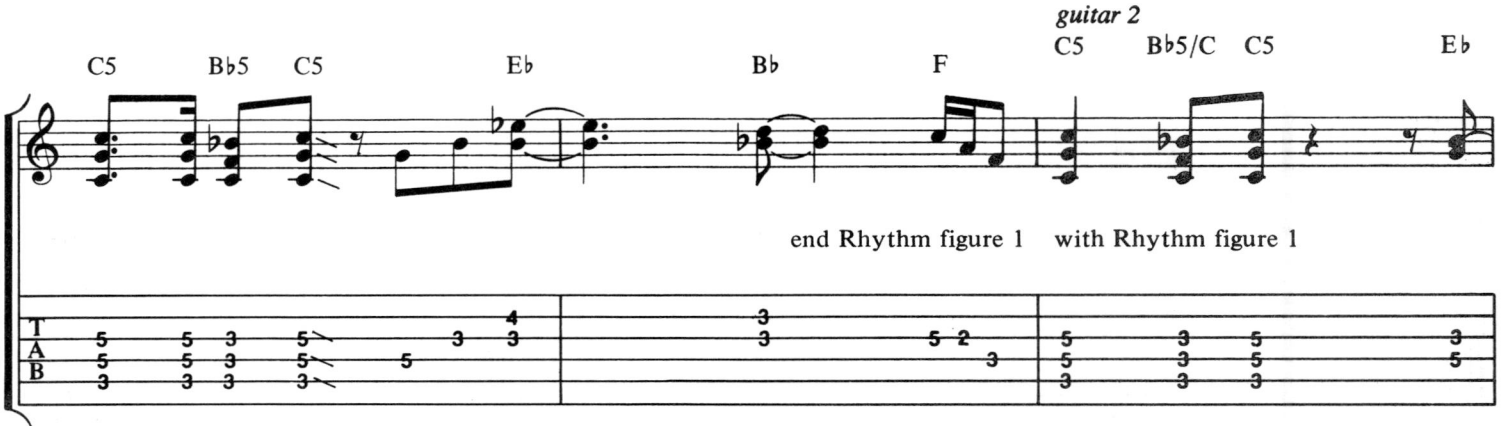

COPYRIGHT © 1986 BY J. ALBERT & SON PTY, LIMITED.
ALL RIGHTS FOR THE U.S. AND CANADA ADMINISTERED BY J. ALBERT & SON (USA) INC., ASCAP.
INTERNATIONAL COPYRIGHT SECURED. ALL RIGHTS RESERVED. USED BY PERMISSION.

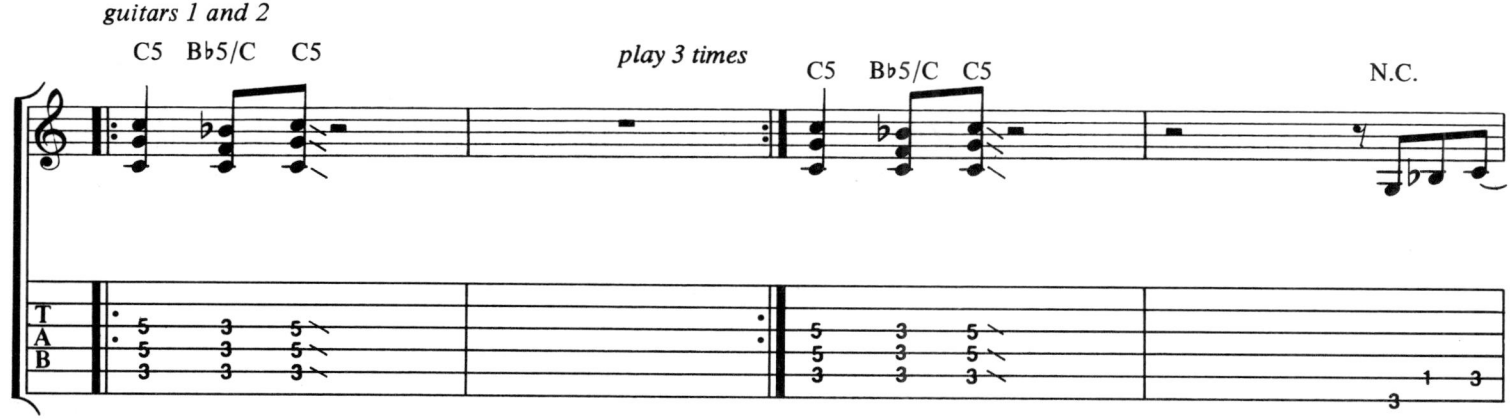

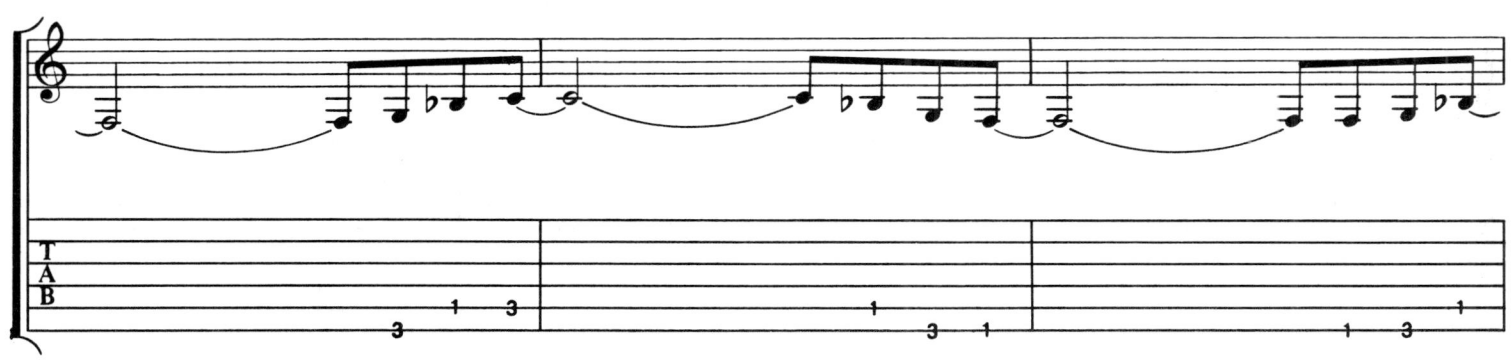
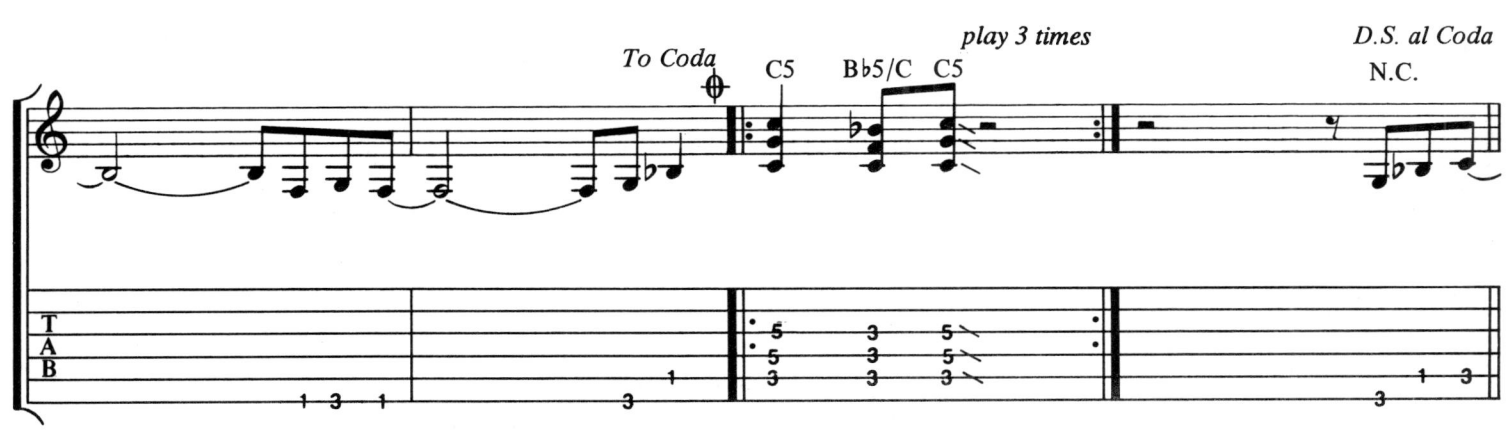

Guitar solo
guitar 1
Coda
C5
Bb5/C
C5
Eb
Bb
F
C5
Bb5/C
C5
Eb
hold bend
guitar 2
Rhythm figure 2
end Rhythm figure 2
with Rhythm figure 1 (1½ times)
with Rhythm figure 2 (3 times)
Bb
F
C5
Bb5/C
C5
Eb
Bb
F
hold bend
hold bend
C5
Bb5/C
C5
Eb
Bb
F

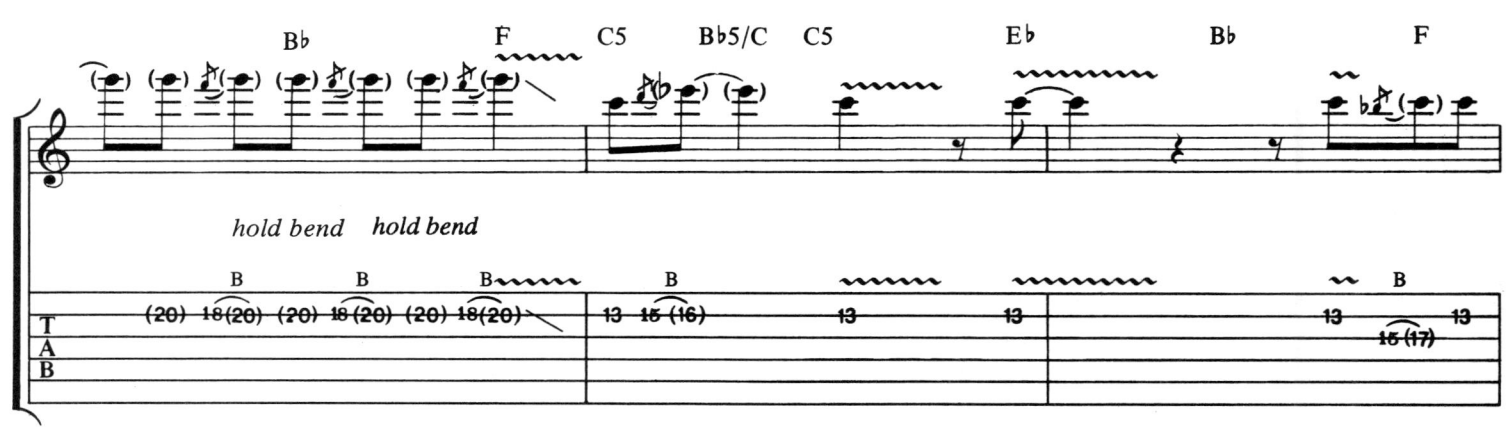

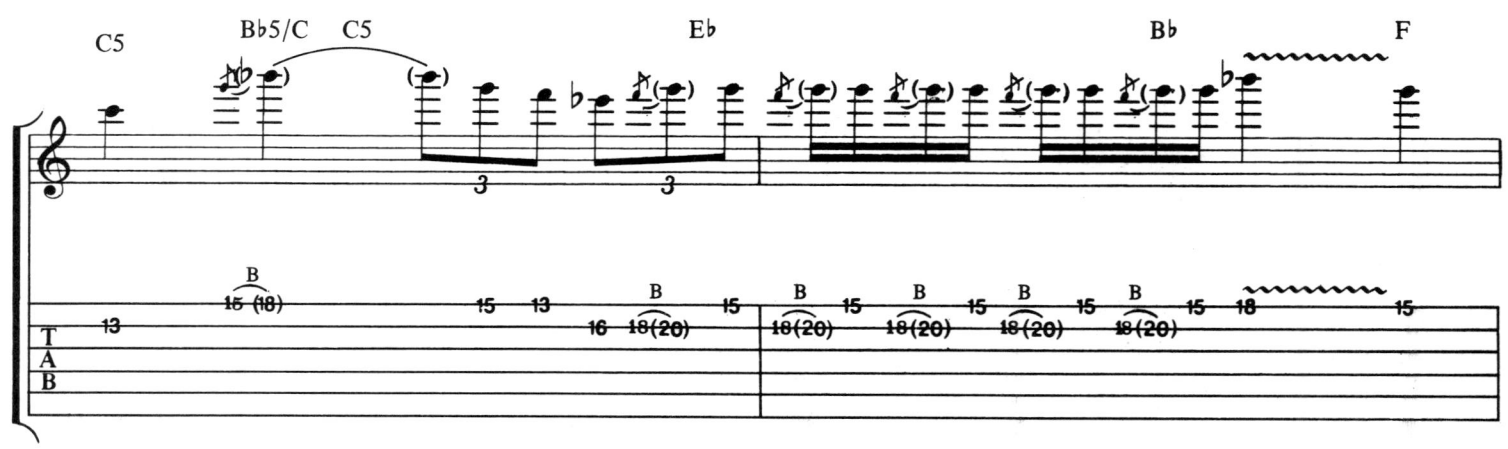

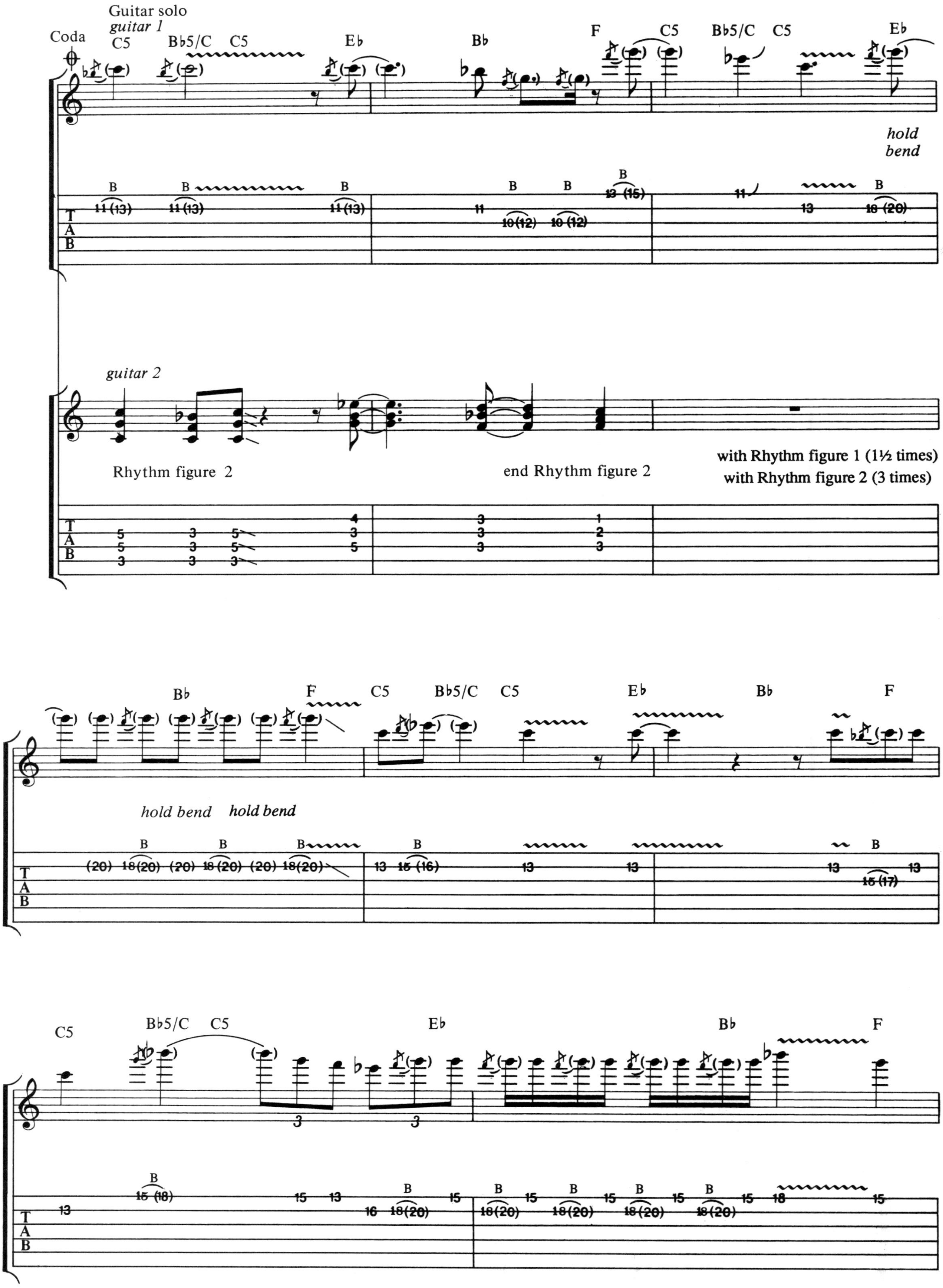

SINK THE PINK

YOUNG/YOUNG/JOHNSON

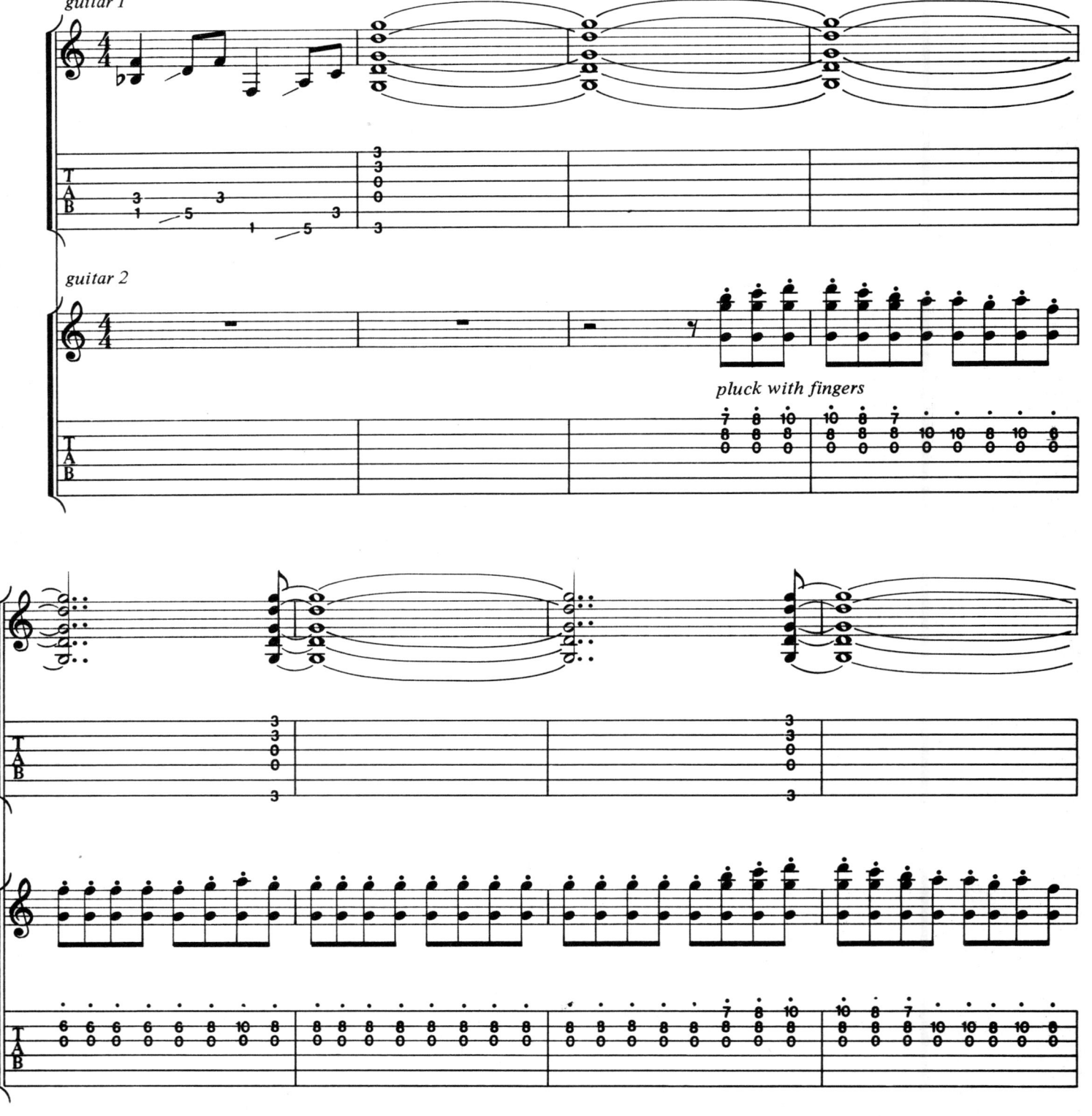

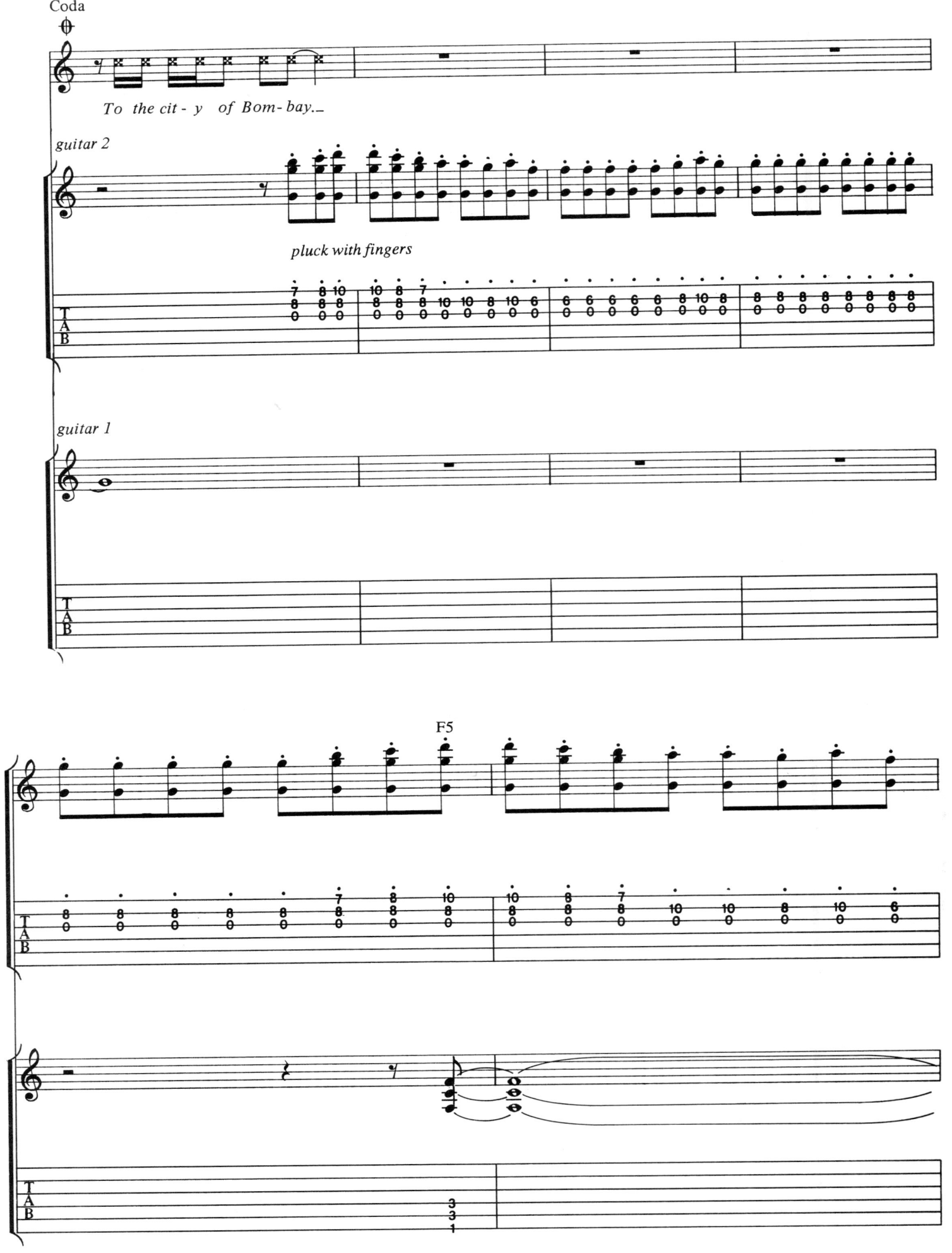

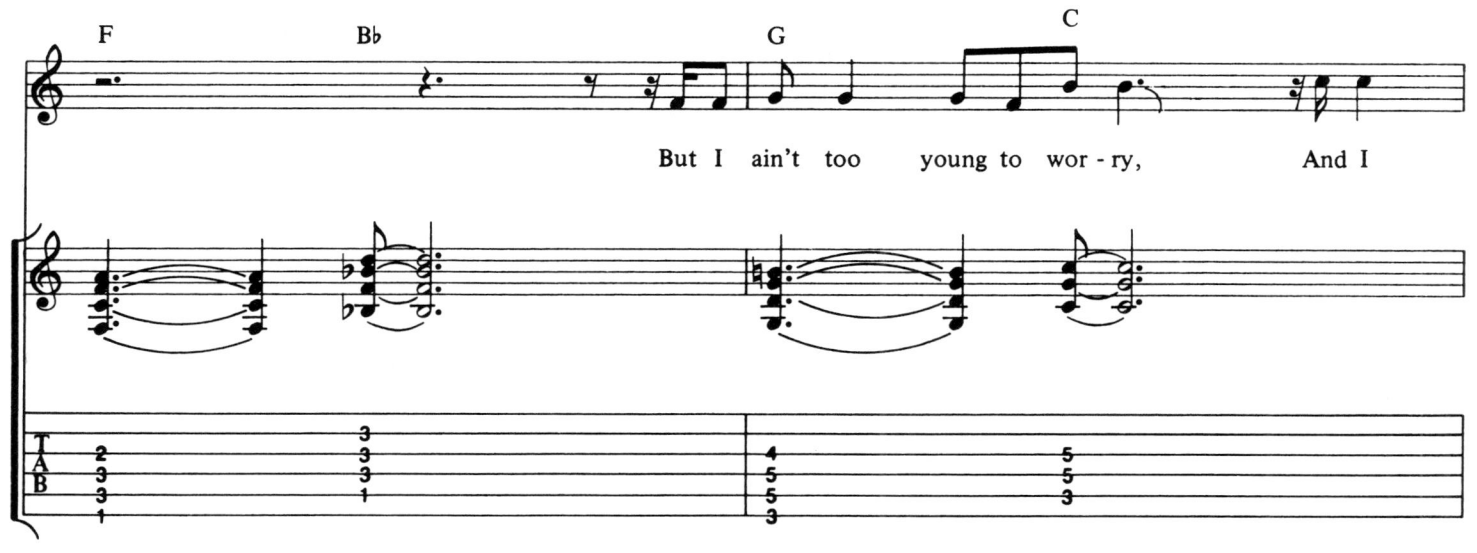
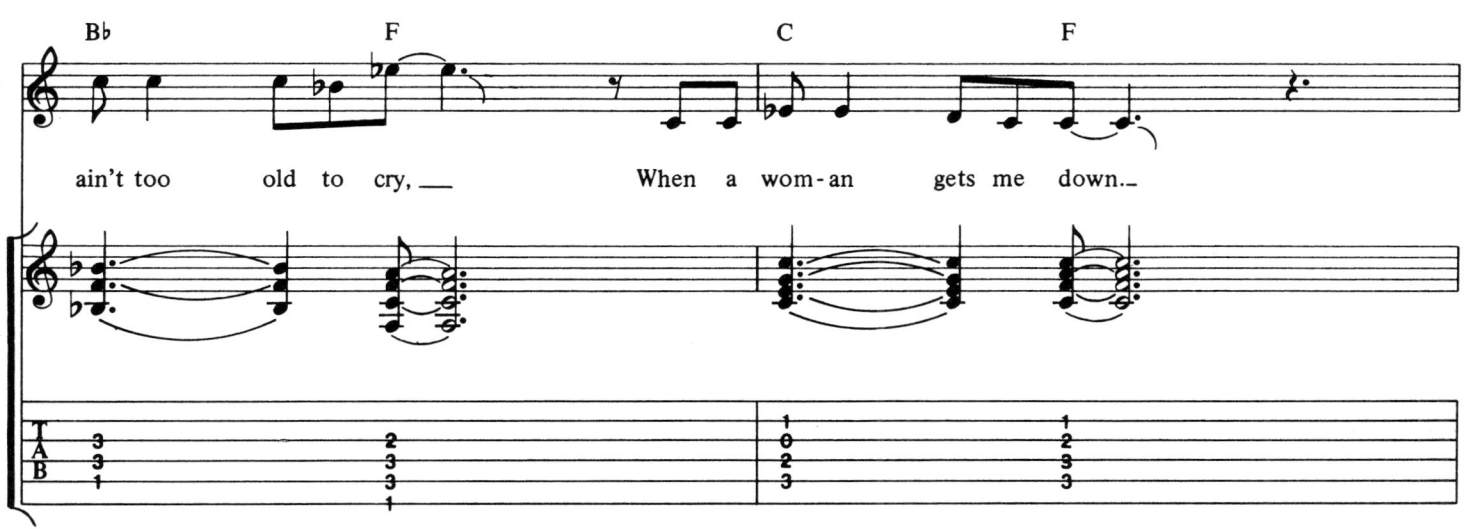
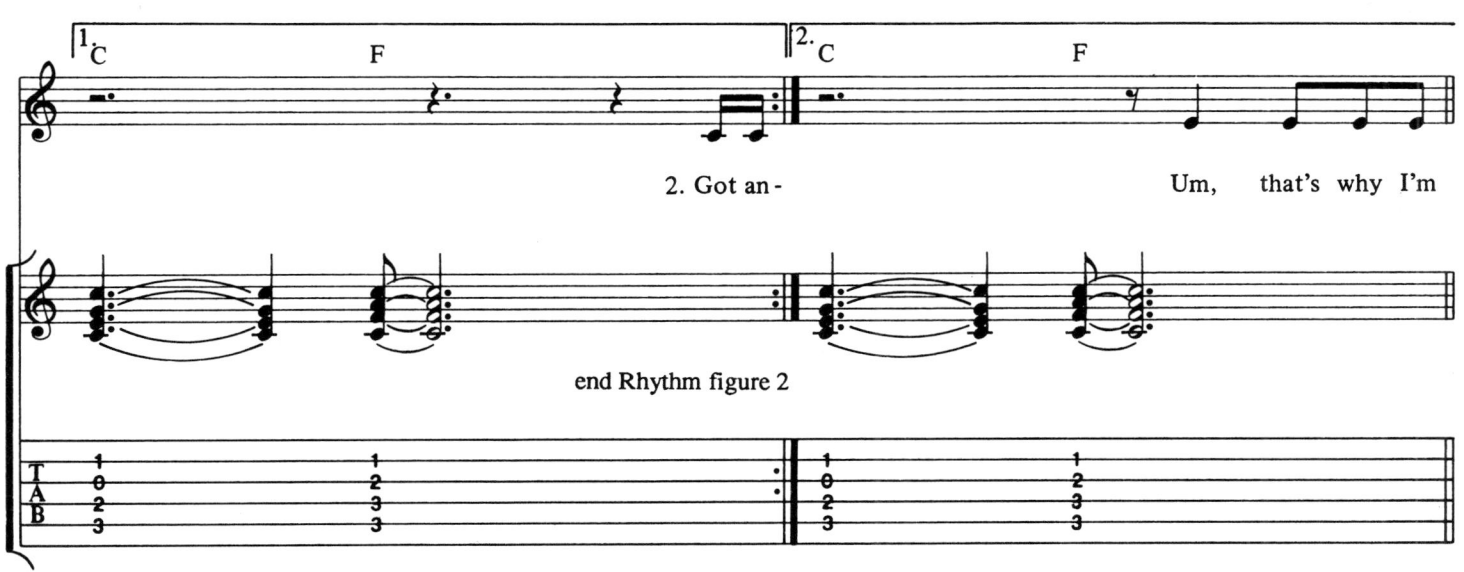

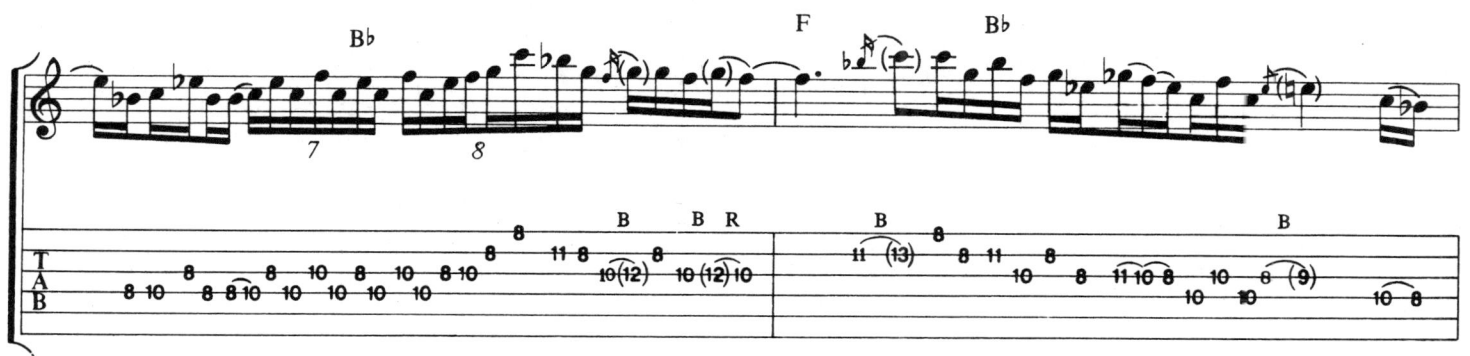

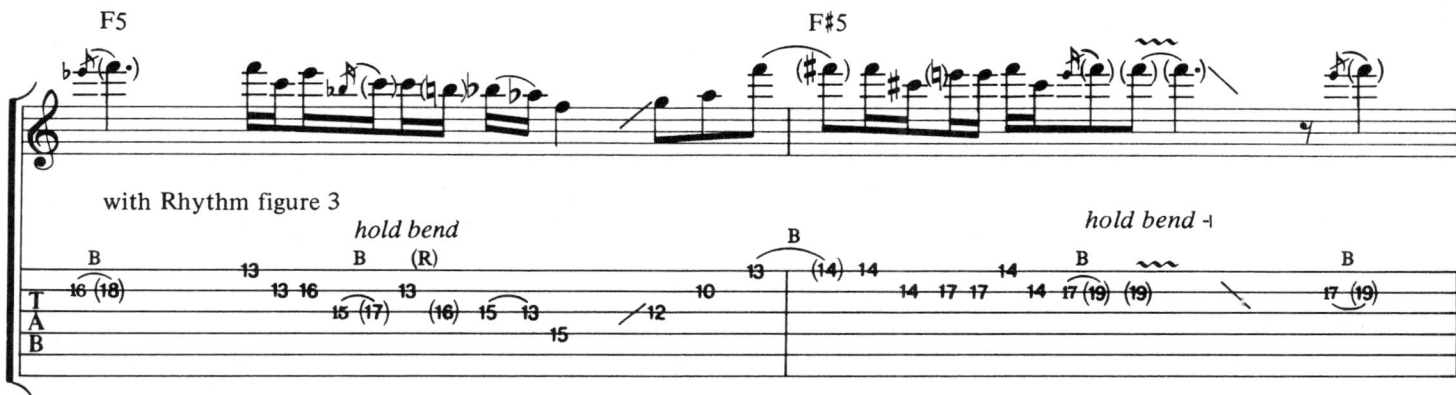
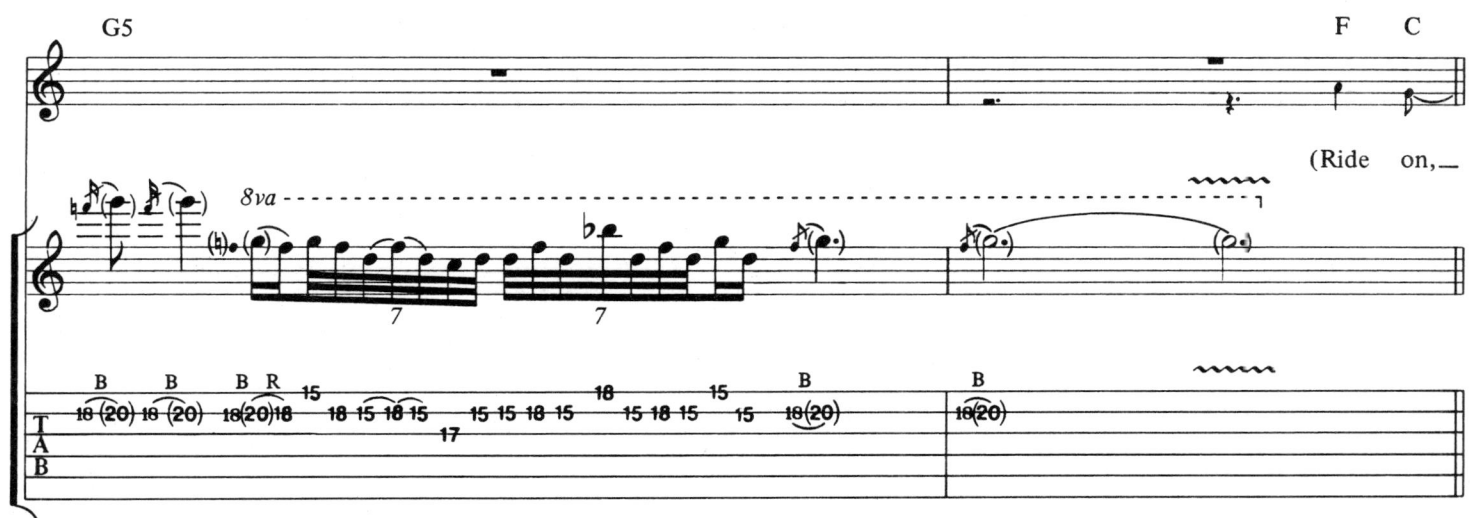

Additional Lyrics

2. Got another empty bottle,
   And another empty bed,
   Ain't too young to admit it,
   And I'm not too old to lie,
   I'm just another empty head.

HELLS BELLS

YOUNG/YOUNG/JOHNSON

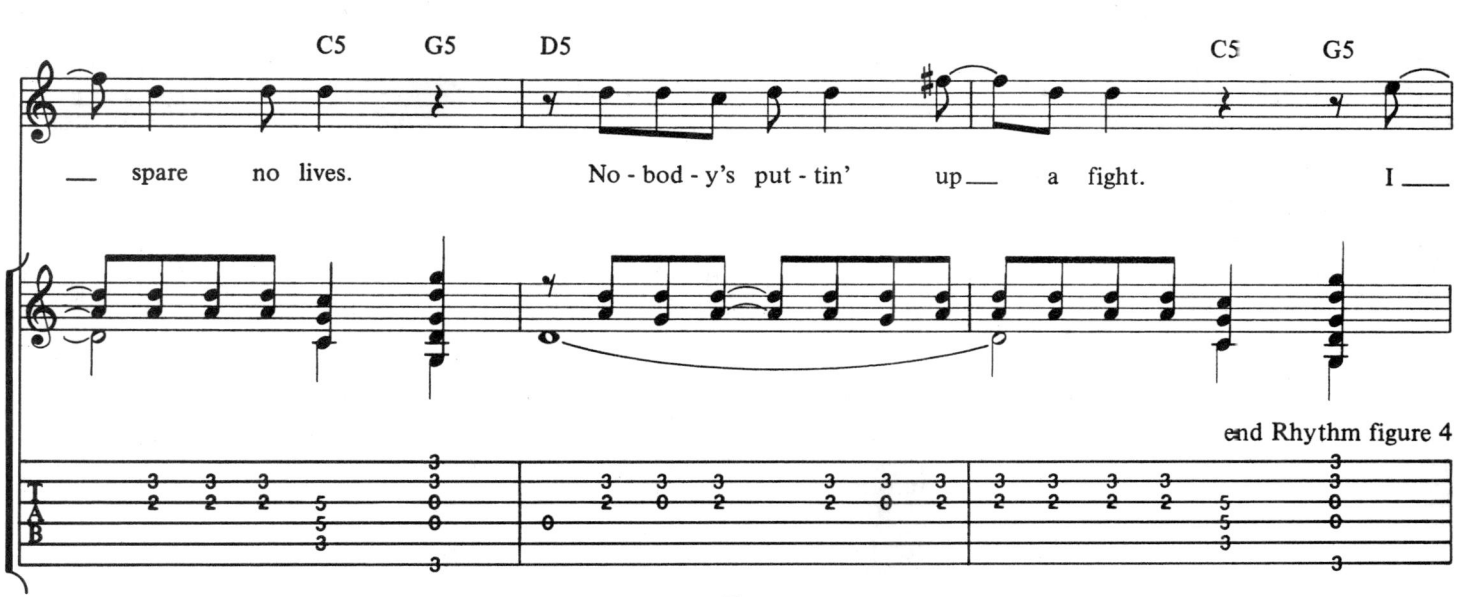

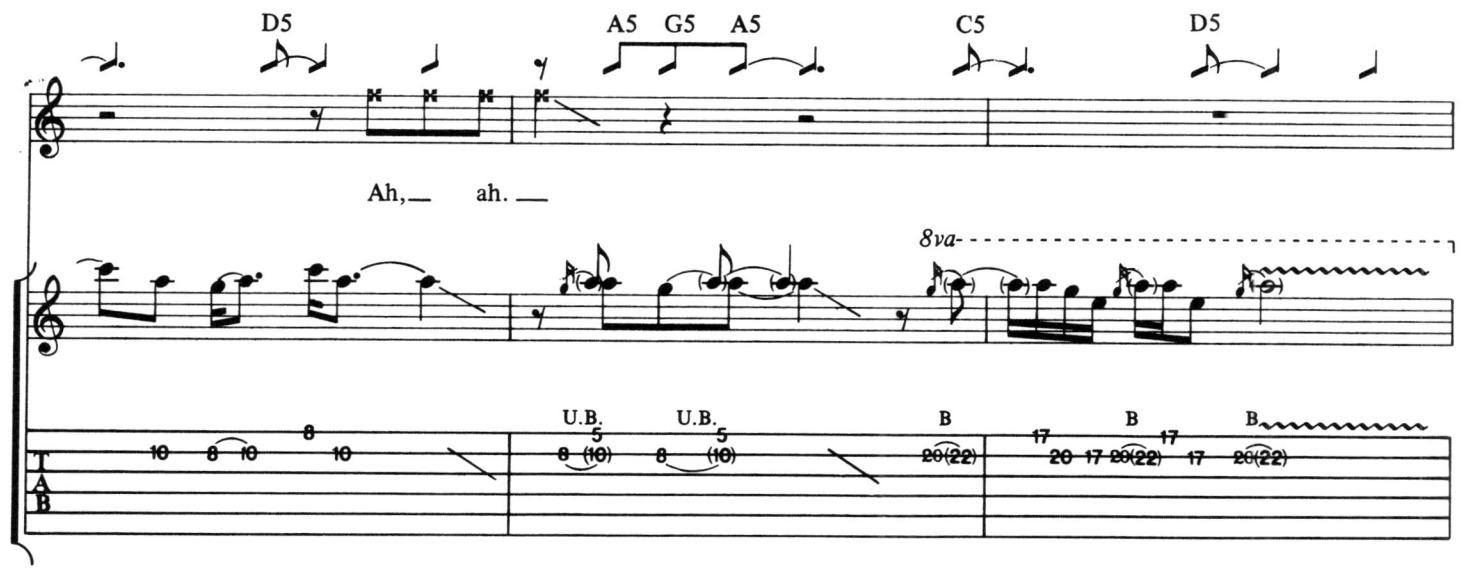

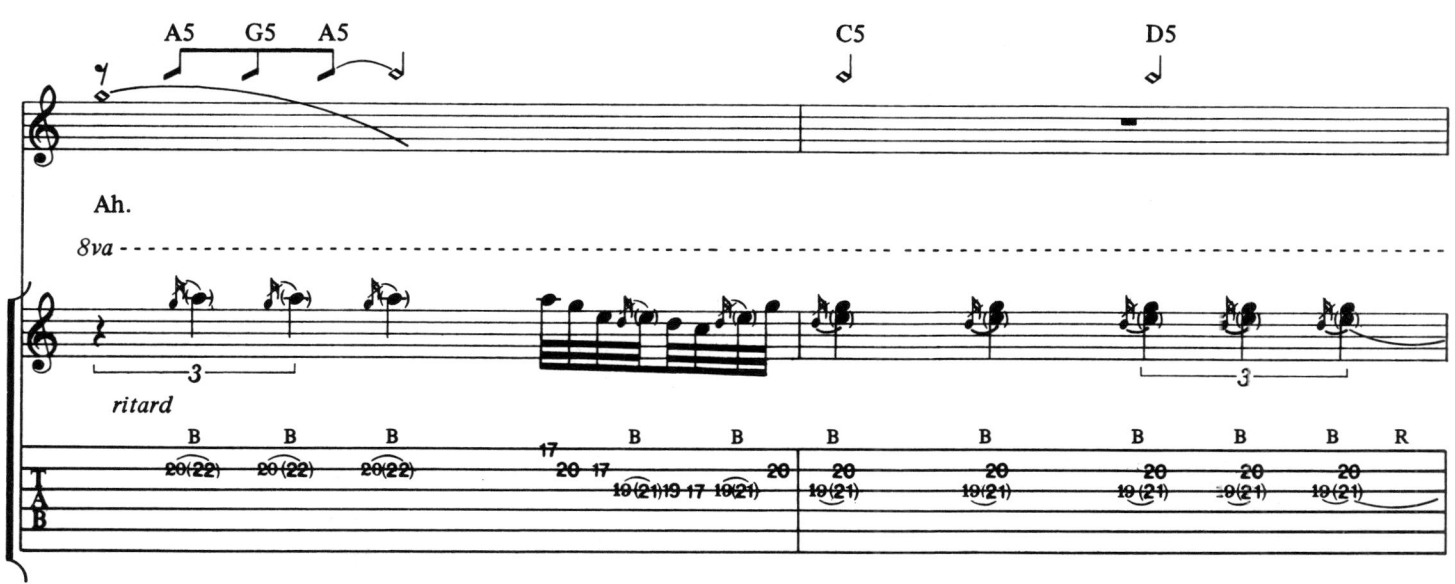

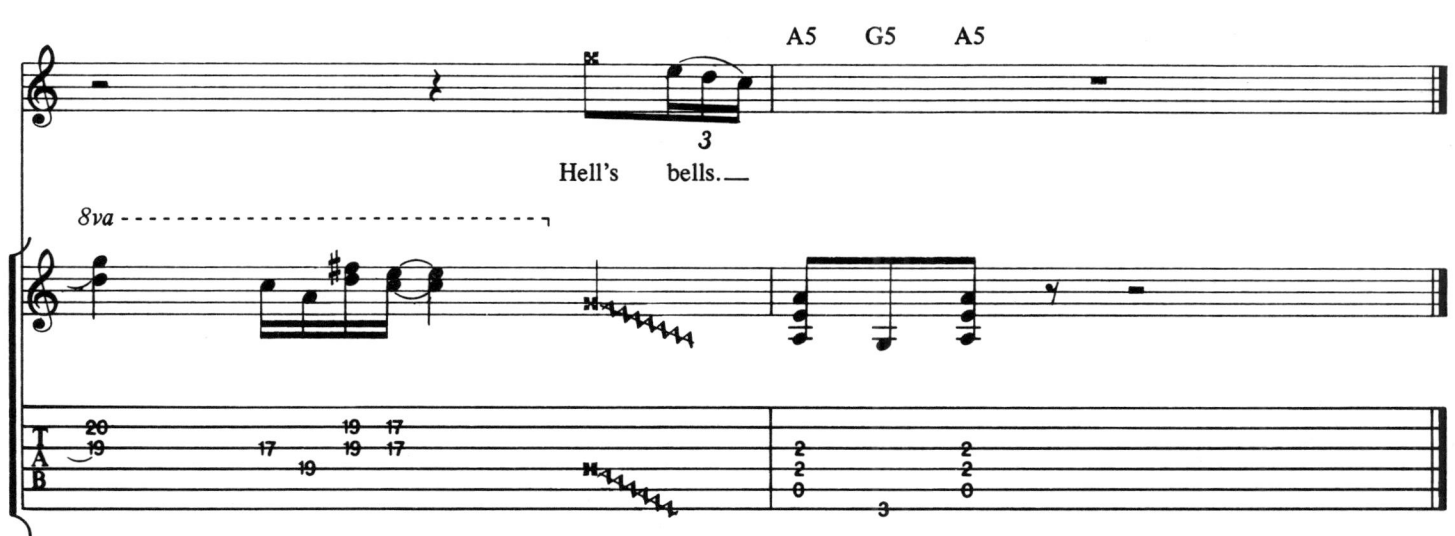

SHAKE YOUR FOUNDATIONS

YOUNG/YOUNG/JOHNSON

COPYRIGHT © 1985 BY J. ALBERT & SON PTY. LIMITED.
ALL RIGHTS FOR THE U.S. AND CANADA ADMINISTERED BY J. ALBERT & SON (USA) INC., ASCAP.
INTERNATIONAL COPYRIGHT SECURED. ALL RIGHTS RESERVED. USED BY PERMISSION.

guitar 2
8va-
D5
G7(no 3rd)
Rhythm figure 4
with Rhythm figure 1 (2 times)
guitar 3
Rhythm figure 4a
1.
2.
G5
G7(no 3rd)
G5
G5
2. I was tak-
end Rhythm figure 4
end Rhythm figure 4a

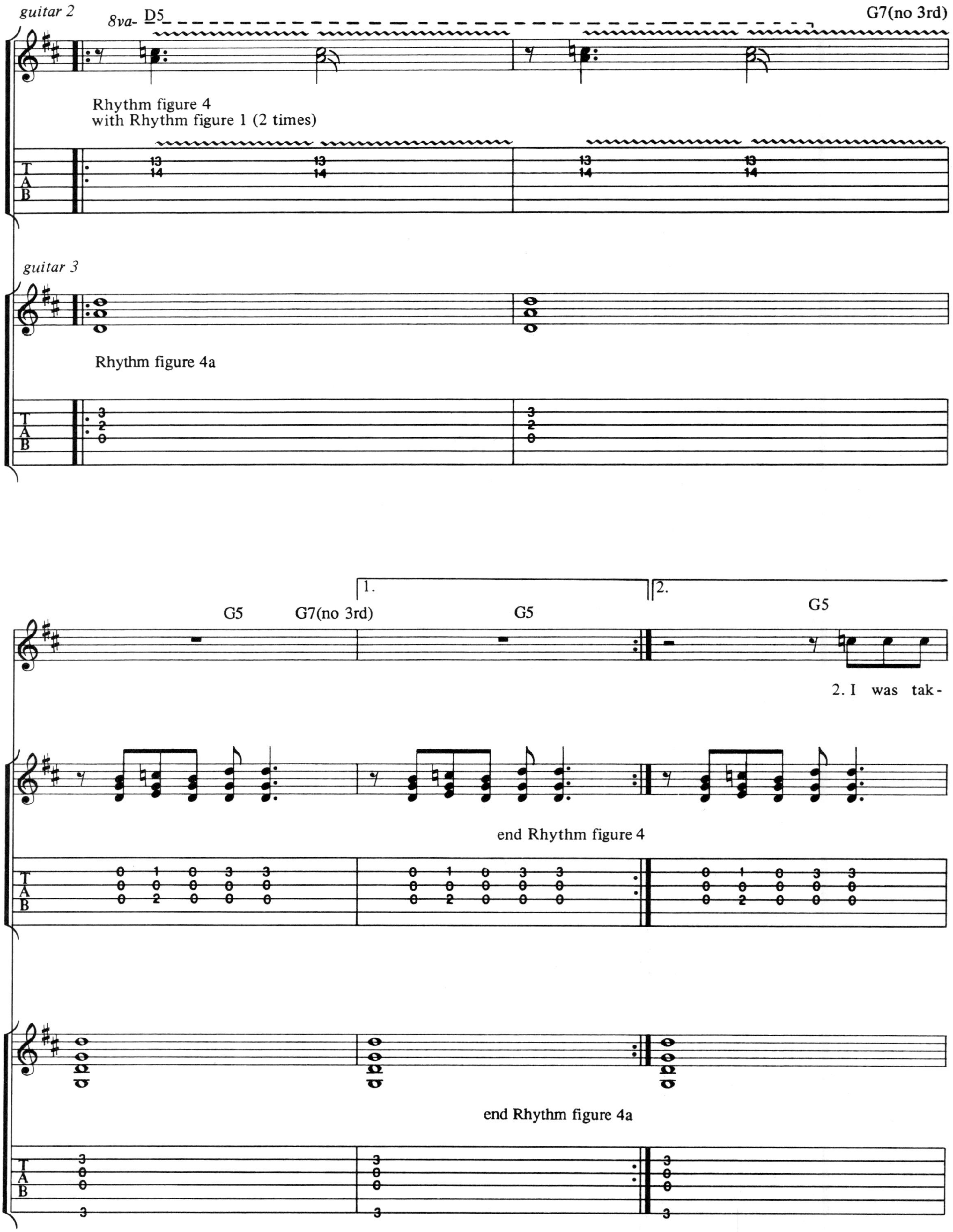

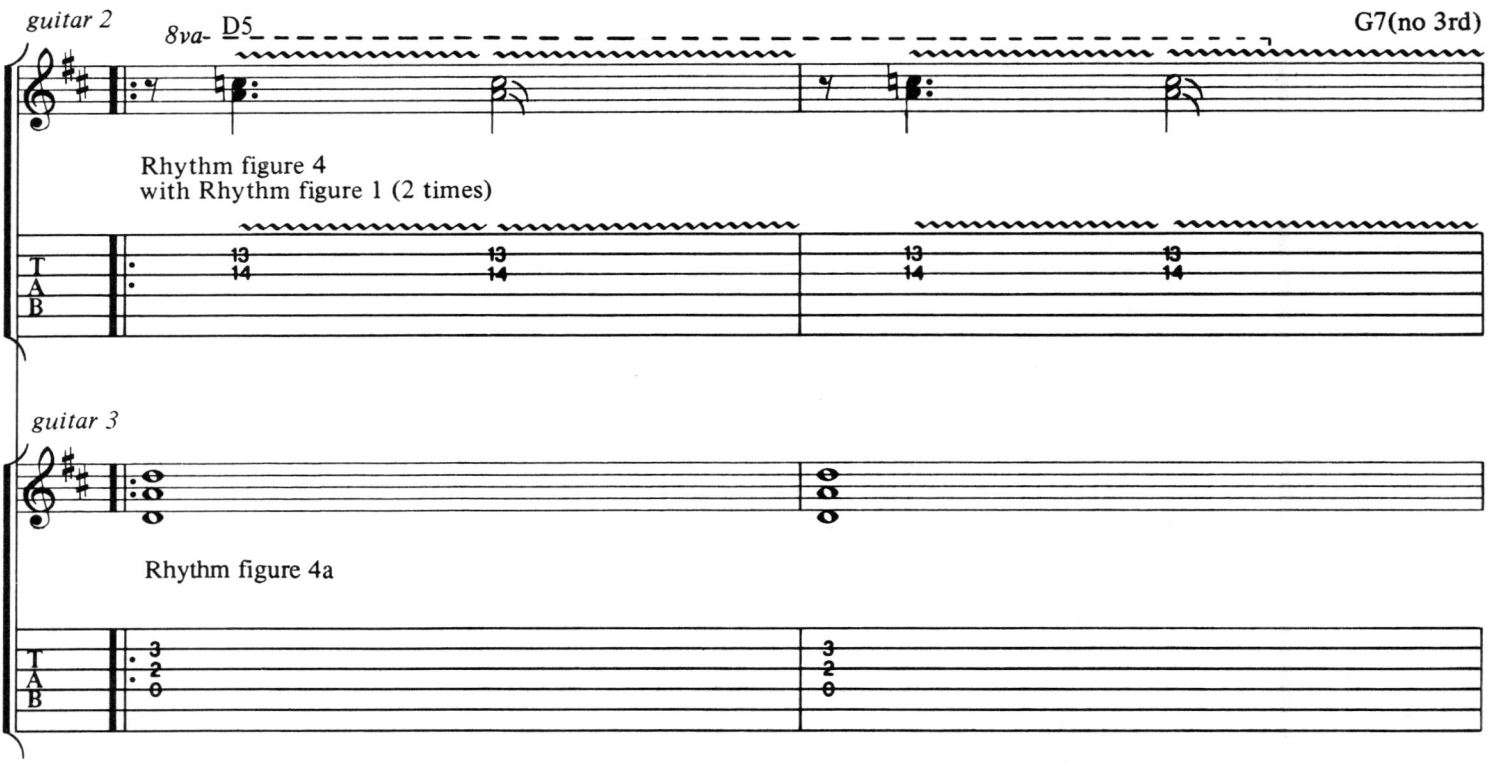

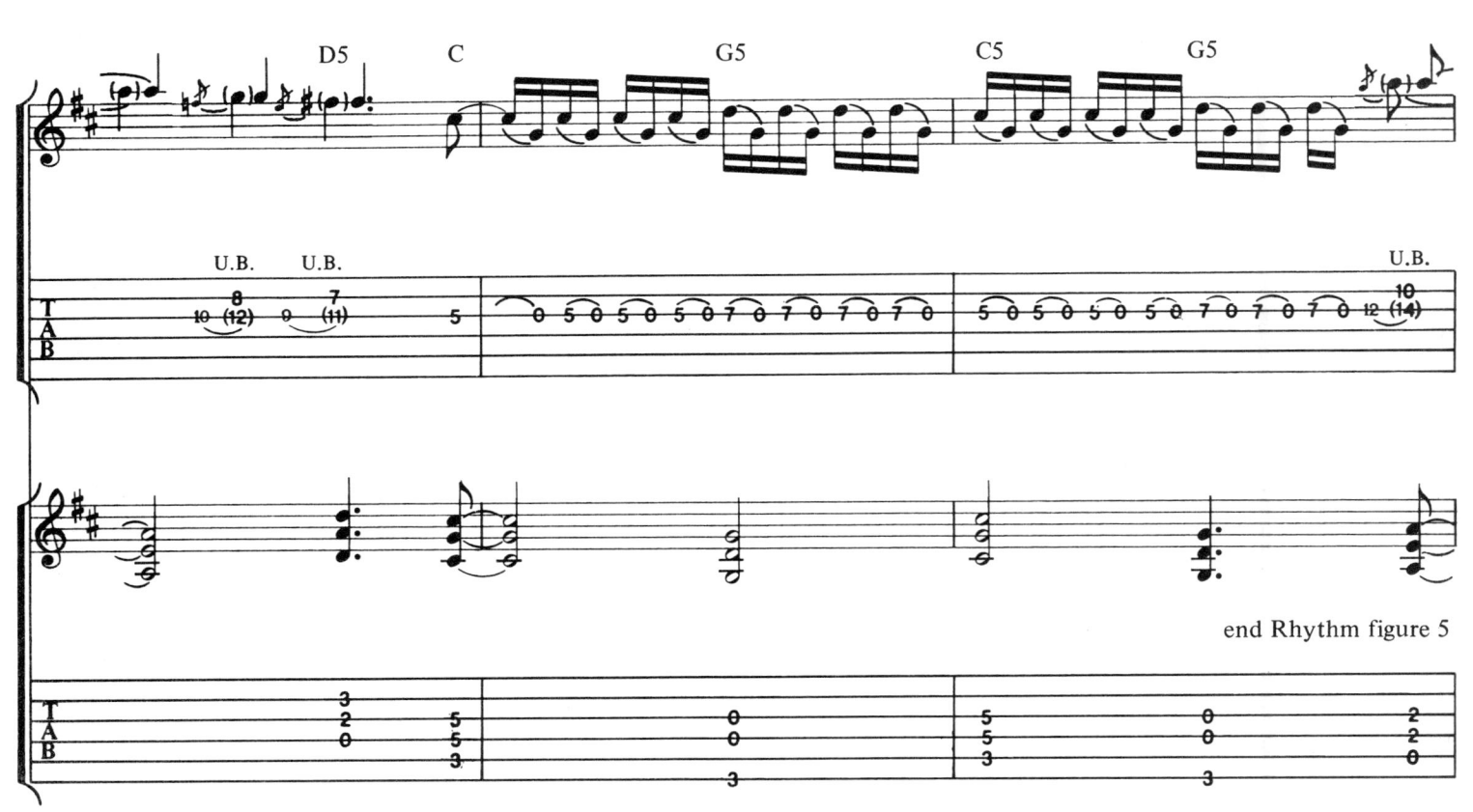

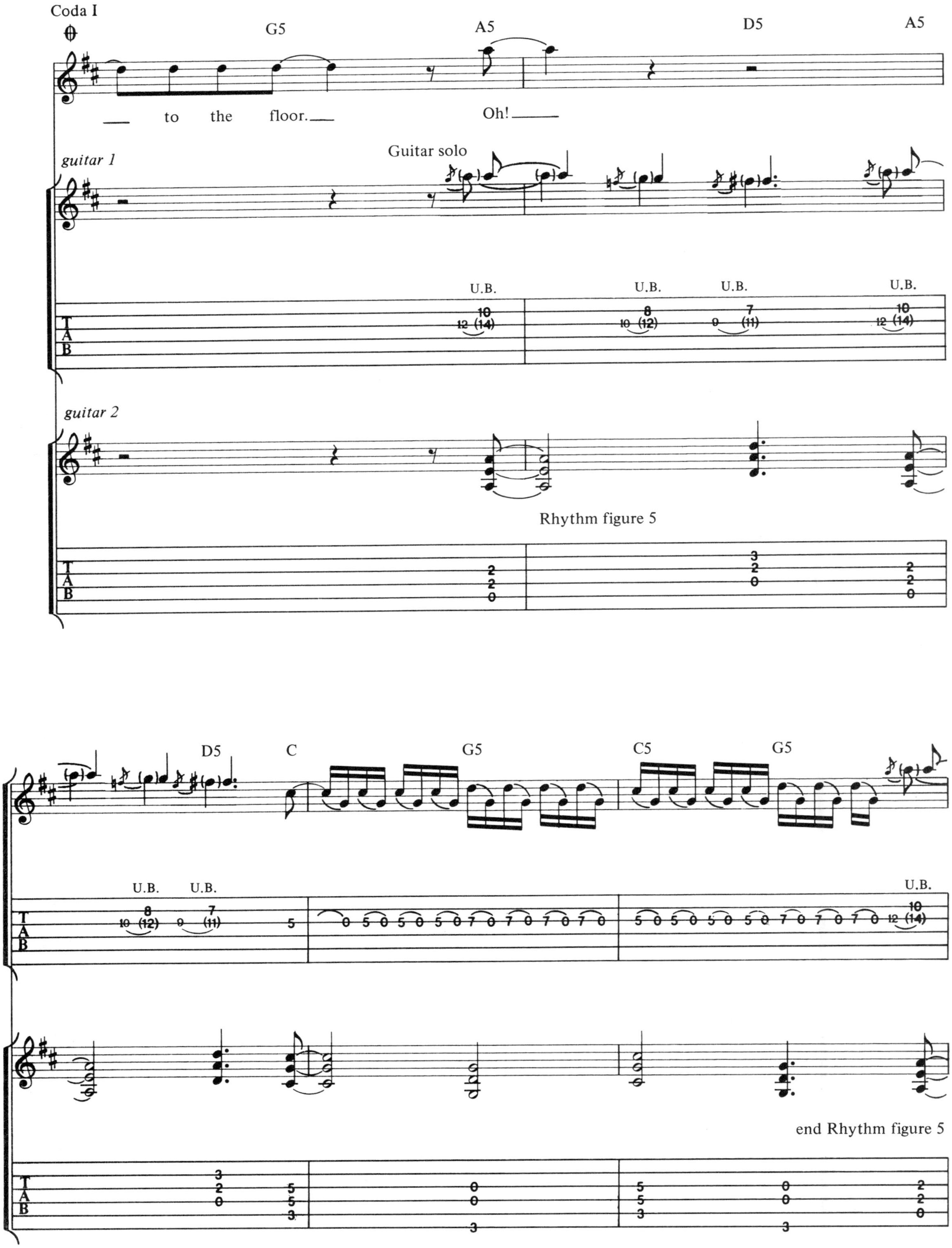
Coda I
G5
A5
D5
A5
— to the floor. —
Oh! —
guitar 1
Guitar solo
U.B.
U.B.
U.B.
U.B.
guitar 2
Rhythm figure 5
D5
C
G5
C5
G5
U.B.
U.B.
U.B.
end Rhythm figure 5

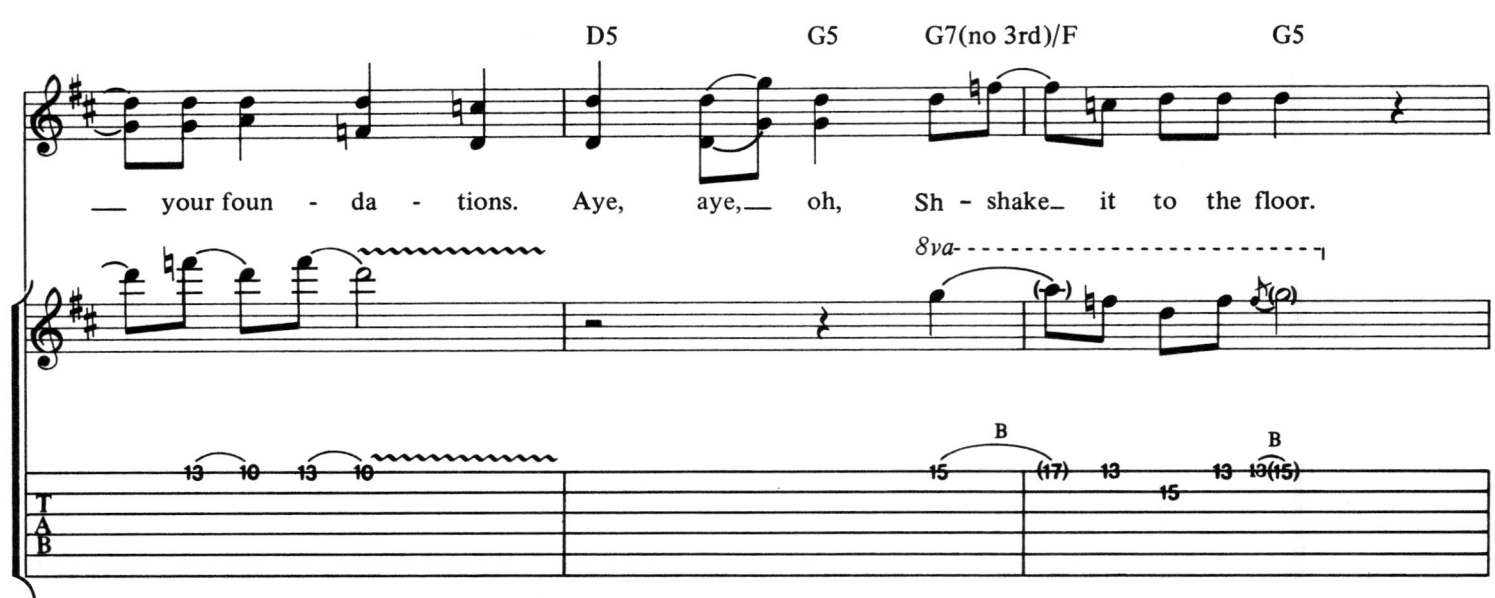

FOR THOSE ABOUT TO ROCK (WE SALUTE YOU)

YOUNG/YOUNG/JOHNSON

COPYRIGHT © 1982 BY J. ALBERT & SON PTY, LIMITED.
ALL RIGHTS FOR THE U.S. AND CANADA ADMINISTERED BY J. ALBERT & SON (USA) INC., ASCAP.
INTERNATIONAL COPYRIGHT SECURED. ALL RIGHTS RESERVED. USED BY PERMISSION.